Coaches Welcome. Young Hilda
Reeves stands in the doorway.

The Lodge
These 100 foot poplars were safely
lopped and felled by teenaged Ian Rose,
under his father's instructions in 1949.

The pond – the Parish Council complained that the cow
slurry was a road hazard. Farmer Jack Costin said "If
you supply cow nappies, I will fit them"!

The water wheel after Bunker's Mill was burnt down in 1923.

Characters of
WOOD,
WURLITZER
& WESLEY

Maurice Sanders looks back

Published in 1990
by
Cortney Publications,
57 Ashwell Street, Ashwell, Baldock, Herts. SG7 5QT

ISBN 0 904378 36 5

Printed by
Henry Ling Limited, Dorchester

ACKNOWLEDGEMENTS

Once more I am indebted to scores of friends who have helped transform the idea of this book into a reality. My thanks and appreciation go to the following:

To all contributors who loaned photographs, and gave me so much time.

To the Association of Professional Foresters, who provided the meeting places for many of the characters herein.

To John Buckledee, for all his help, and permission to copy 'Luton News' photographs.

To Maureen Clarke and Bob Macfee, who gave me access to the Bedford archives.

To Hilda Stronach who co-ordinated the entire James Jones Story.

To Ben Hinton, ex Royal Marine and Foden devotee. His massive ground work research doesn't show on the surface, yet he has held the key to many timber folk and ferried photographs hundreds of miles for your delight, in all my books. His friendship, inspiration, support and kindnesses to me are valued beyond any words of mine.

To Bill Walker and Peter Allen, whose tremendous efforts have made so much of the Organ story possible. Particularly Peter, who put me in touch with Harvey Roehl of the Vestal Press, New York, the only holder of the Reginald Foort Commer Van photographs known to me. This amazing American cousin waived copyright fees, and wished me well with the project.

To various members of the Theatre, and Cinema Organ Clubs, who helped, particularly Frank Hare, who went to so much trouble. Also to Laurie Morley, who I have never met, yet from whom I have received so many Foort facts, and many hours of organ tapes.

To Dr. David Shaw, M.A., who for a contribution to the Dialect Atlas of England and Scotland, travelled throughout Bedfordshire recording hours of local characters in the 1950s, from which I gleaned many unknown facts.

To Peter Mayne, good friend and local historian, who has done so much to nurture and assist with old Eaton Bray facts and details. His vast collection of slides and memorabilia is of incalculable heritage value. Plus the host of local folk, who have given unstintingly of their time and memories.

To the Rev. Dr. Donald English of the Methodist Church Home Mission Division, Paul Lang, Cedric Bush, and Morris Walker, who dipped into the archives for the Mobile Cinema photographs for me.

To my wife, Helen, for her dexterity with our well thumbed dictionary.

To Joyce Baker, who undertook the marathon task of typing every word of the manuscript from my shocking long hand, and many alterations. A formidable task, carried out with great patience.

To Norman Gurney, my Publisher, Editor, gentle critic, and friend, who occasionally winces at my expressions yet tactfully makes changes acceptable to me, and palatable to the reader; coping with my ailing health and literary limitations, yet producing quality books that have won acclaim in a specialist subject, to the astonishment of many.

Again, to all these, my most sincere thanks.

My sweet taste of success is due in part to a variety of outlets, some quite unorthodox.

Will the following Individuals, Clubs, and Societies, please accept my warmest appreciation: the Lads at 'Latil Lodge', Mike Miller, Anthony Fielding, Chris Evans and George Fensom. Keith Shakespeare and his wife and the host of young people who man the National Traction Engine Club Bookstands across the U.K.; Derrick Bishop of the I.O.W. Railway Society. The various groups within the National Vintage Tractor and Engine Club. Pat and Mrs. Treadway - Chiltern Branch Historic Commercial Vehicle Society. Mr. & Mrs. Steve Wimbush, who gave SORTH such a magnificent launch in the Commercial Vehicle and Road Transport Club. 'Wheels and Tracks', a Journal that has taken my name overseas. Landsman's Mobile Books, who have done me so well at Smithfield and County Shows. Albion Scott and Russell Jones Books amazed me, but top world wide sales go to Mr. & Mrs. Robin Pearson of Nynehead Books. (How did you do it?)

In the timber trade Scottish Woodlands (Argyll) efforts are most noteworthy, as are those of our leading Forestry Mail Order Companies: Stuart (Broadleaf) Brown, who first gambled SORTH on an unknown market; Michael and Shirley Richmond, who started selling chainsaws when injury stopped Michael using them; the current flourishing cottage-born business once almost packed every room; Stanton Hope, who in 1954 would sharpen and return post a saw chain for a shilling or two, for amateurs like me. Honey Brothers, who can claim "We try it before you buy it" in tree surgery at home and abroad. Finally, newcomer John Venables, has made his mark. All your effort have been works of supererogation! Look it up - I had to. (*So did I. Editor*)

Well done.

CONTENTS

INTRODUCTION

This is the last of my four books, and as the title implies, it is more of an autobiographical nature than its predecessors - a recollection of days of mine, and of others, now long since gone. It is a blending of the experiences of fascinating people, most of whom I have come to know. In widening my timber horizons there are glimpses of rare characters, some of whom have moulded my life in and around my native village of Eaton Bray in Bedfordshire - a place now seen by some inhabitants as a 'memorial to greed' where the influx of the affluent has out-numbered the 'peasants', as someone once called us.

My Publisher described this book as a 'mish mash' of Motors, Music and Methodism, which just about sums up my life.

Those who have prevailed upon me to write in this way should remember that local references must be of interest to all my readers, who will in turn, I trust, warm to glimpses of a country lad's surroundings. One thing remains unchanged. It is another book of worthy characters I have chosen to honour. To write four acceptable books in five years is gratifying, if exhausting. A reviewer praised my work, then added 'people would not buy my books to improve their English', and that I seemed more of a 'doer' than a writer. My life has been with some whose I.Q. is so low it would not register on any scale. Brilliant Timbermen, who signed their name with an X. Several even today write all their letters via the telephone! A degree in English Literature is of little help when one is stuck over the axles in mud! In contrast, an educated Forestry Officer wrote commending the heritage value of these valiant workers' stories. I'm better at splitting wood than infinitives! At least I write myself, and not through a hired professional. Ill health cost me two years of schooling, but I enjoyed writing. I suffered the ignominy of being made to stand up in class as my teacher read from my well intended, if atrocious, efforts, pausing like a comedian for the laughter. I am not a 9 to 5 writer. Inspiration comes at the oddest times, like 'at traffic lights' or in the 'check-out' at Sainsburys. There are two ways to write a book: the easy way, and mine. Seeking, searching, and listening across the country, which profits the GPO and British Telecom more than me.

Like the bumble bee who, according to the law of aerodynamics, cannot fly due to its weight to wing span ratio, yet blissfully unaware of these facts goes about his business, I, in turn, lack all the skills of writers, yet have had the good fortune to enjoy success.

In the 1960s I was lopping a tree perched on top of an excavator jib, when a gust of wind took me and a branch 20 feet down, fracturing two vertebrae. Four different hospital specialists declared my days in timber were over. Helen, and a wonderful part-time man named Jim, kept me going through the misery and despair of back pain.

In 1981 I met a sports injury specialist, Craig Simmons, who invited me to his clinic on a 'no help-no charge' basis. He got to work on uninjured muscles and in two months I was climbing and chainsawing in the tree tops again. I had not seen Craig in 30 years. The tousled-haired little lad who had given me the run-around in Youth Club was to hold the key to my business, health, and hope. A gift top medics could not offer.

Helen came to our camp as a NAAFI Manageress, and I drank gallons of NAAFI tea (a known health hazard) getting to know her. One time sleeping 12 girls in 8 beds pushed together, she knew something of wartime deprivations. Firemen were still hoseing gutted Putney Methodist Church as I drove past, four days before we were to be wed there in 1944. A kindly Baptist Minister did the nuptials, as Flying Bombs fell all around his Church.

This Derby-born forces sweetheart bore and raised our three daughters, one sadly handicapped.

Somehow she roped trees, humped organs, kept the books of both businesses, and coped with a partner despondent from nagging spinal pain. Serving coffee with a smile up to midnight to potential organ customers, after a day's monkey winching, is a fair test of a good marriage!

This book is dedicated to the Men and Women who have been, or still are, the life blood of our timber trade, and kindred types in society in general. Perhaps even you, Reader?

Our future legacy to Youth must include the teaching of true values. Evidence of our magnificent young people abounds today but is not considered newsworthy.

This is a book of characters I consider are!!!

When I was a boy a song topped the charts "There's a good time coming, be it ever so far away". For some it never came.

In the 1920s a Radio Entertainer named Stanelli had a variety act playing tunes on an array of motor horns he called his 'Hornchestra', and I would identify Lucas and other makes. My love of music and motors is that old. My world of WurliTzer organs was mostly a profit-making hobby, if one counts the hours, but most music is fun, and that is what we sold to scores of folk. Some are friends today.

As our attention turns to tomorrow's world, we must be mindful of its inheritors. When I felled a tree at a Home for Disturbed Children, two fascinated eight or nine-year olds claimed to have seen the "Chainsaw Massacre" video many times. 'How long would it take you to saw up a human body' they seriously enquired. Cutting wood was to them a new chainsaw application!! Hence a glimpse of some of the stalwarts of an older generation who have served the youth of their day.

The ensuing deprivation and camaraderie of 1939 is not soon forgotten. During the last war, every stick of timber was controlled, and licensed. There were thousands of tons of wood required alone for Mulberry Harbour, some of which was growing two days before becoming shuttering. A village carpenter, who applied for sufficient wood for coffins for the following winter, was asked to be more precise. He quietly visited every pensioner, did his own health check, then wrote back "about 15, if it's a bad winter"! A farmer applied for a licence for a new pig sty, and was promptly told to build a brick one. His indignant reply - "I note your instructions. How does one make a brick door, please"?

Meanwhile the Yanks were unloading their first 3,000 tons of tractor and excavator spares on an airfield, and were burning an estimated 1,000 tons of packing cases with 2 Cat D8s. Their Colonel was desperate. "Get me 50 truck loads of goddam shelving" he urged my Major. Tactfully, Uncle Sam's Army were reminded that this was the U.K. with her back to the wall, but we could help. A telephone call brought 50 saws (hand), 150 hammers, and half a ton of mixed nails. As for the wood, build with it, instead of burning it, was the advice!!

After the war probably no other industry has 'beat swords into ploughshares' like the timber trade. Apart from all the adapted vehicles, the range ran from ex W.D. axes (hand for the use of), to the two ex 'D' Day floating units of Mulberry Harbour - 'demobbed' and developed into pierheads by Phoenix Timber Co. Ltd on the Thames at Rainham, Essex. Today, even logs are fed into sawmills from a conveyor made of joined lengths of Bren Gun Carrier track.

From the hoards of yarns, here are two about 'The Guvnor'. A plane crashed and caught fire in a field close to a Unipower. As the driver ran, and heroically drove the scorched tractor to safety, the Boss, mindful of the insurance, chided him with "No, you fool, drive it in nearer"!! Another Unipower overturned just after being refuelled. As her driver crawled clear, with a lacerated back drenched with battery acid, his 'Guvnor' greeted him with 'never mind your back, get a can down and catch all that Derv running away'!! The calibre of men found in our trade is encapsulated in a fellow who motor cycled half across Scotland with a Fordson cylinder head on his back. Each time the holding rope almost throttled him he would stop and rest the head on a wall or gate post.

Next time you admire Ian Sparks' gorgeously restored Foden 'D' type Tractor AMB 300 at a rally, think of sprightly 83-year old Frederick Pratt of Umberleigh, Devon, who drove her from new in 1933 for James Murch and Sons. He shifted huge loads all over Devon, including massive trees into Dartington Hall sawmills, Totnes, once in snow in June, he tells me. His claim to fame is when the boxer, Carnea Hercules, was training for his title fight. Fred hauled the elm that made the clubs for his training. The timberman is the uncrowned king of innovators, committed to a way of life that is the hallmark of ingenuity, stubbornness, and dedication to an on-going fight with the natural elements - a self-reliant breed that take on Big Trees, Big Tractors, and Big Bank Managers.

In this, my last gathering of 'giants', who have blazed a trail lesser men would shrink from, I have weaved others of Bedfordshire, Organs, and yes, even Methodism!

ABOUT THE PHOTOGRAPHS

The major feature of this book is the photographs, almost all never published before. Many are treasured snapshots that lose their quality on enlargement, yet are of unique vehicles, loads, and situations; priceless reminders men and women have of their prime. Some have been proudly carried in drivers' wallets, thus making the fold marks which cannot be erased. Some were dog-eared, ravaged by time, sun, heat, dirt, and damp.

Again I have to say my books are never intended as collections of super photographs, but rather a visual evidence and insight into the lives of some remarkable people: amateur snapshots yes, but everyone of them someone's prized gems. Once again my good friend, Dave Gillow, undertook the colossal task of copying over 300 prints in all.

Undaunted he coped with misfocused snapshots, some on faded cheap colour film in earlier days. The end result of his skills is superb! I am indebted to both Dave and his wife, Carol, who suffered countless calls and inconveniences, on my behalf.

Dave's artistry is best summed up by the wife of an old timberman, who said - "He's never read a book until yours, and as for those pictures, he relives them for hours"!

*Dave's
dexterity*

*Maurice's
delight!*

655 WKX (new to T.T.B.). Richard Berger hauls 900 cube from Widecombe in the Moor, Devon.

GLOSSARY

A.P.F. – Association of Professional Foresters.

ANCHORS – A large spade or sprag, mounted generally on the rear of a tractor to hold the machine whilst roping.

ARTIC – Articulated vehicle.

ALLIS CHALMERS – Make of American Tractor.

A CHANCER – One who takes chances. Not long for the world of timber.

'C' HOOK – A hardened hook shaped like a letter 'C'.

CATS – Caterpillar Tractor Models D2 - D4 - D6 - D7 - D8.

CLEATS OR SPUDS – Various metal bars for extra traction in wet conditions.

COGS – Slang for gears.

CUBE – A cubic foot of round timber assessed by the use of the HOPPUS measure, used by Timbermen for over 100 years. 25 cubic feet of green hardwood weigh about a ton.

CHOCKERMAN – One who hooks up a chain or rope.

CHEV. – Chevrolet - make of lorry.

DED – Dutch Elm Disease.

GRUBBER OR ROOTER – The process of grubbing up trees by their roots.

KETTLE WEDGE – Large wood chip axed out by fallers.

MONKEY WINCH – Powerful hand winch, very slow, very sure.

MMM – "Men, Mud and Machines", a previous book by the Author (still available)

NAAFI – Navy, Army, & Airforce Institute.

QUAD – Light ex-Army Gun Tractor.

QL – Four wheel drive Bedford Army Lorry.

RUDDINGTON, NOTTS – One of the better known places of ex WD Army vehicles sales in the 1950s-60s.

SKIDS and 3 LEGS – Methods of loading timber.

SNATCH BLOCK – Pulley for increasing pull.

SHEFFIELD BLIGHT – Severely lopped tree (steel butchery).

SORTH – Stories of Round Timber Haulage - a previous book by the Author, now sadly out of print.

SPARROW BLINDER – Rough cut hedge.

TRACE HORSE – A horse used as an extra for pulling large loads.

TWITCH, WRISTER OR WITTERING STICK – Names for methods of binding on loads of timber.

TPO – Tree Preservation Order.

TVO – Tractor Vapourising Oil.

TUSHING or SNIGGING – Term for extracting or pulling out trees to point of loading.

WIND THROW – A whole area of gale blown trees.

WIDOW MAKER – A loose broken branch lodged in a tree.

WOODPECKER – A poor axeman.

4 x 4 – A four wheel drive vehicle, likewise **6 x 6.**

ORGANS

CONSOLE – Where the Organist sits at the keyboards, detached from the works. (Often mounted on a lift in cinemas in the days of silent films.)

MANUAL – The name given to an organ keyboard. Numbered one to seven in the U.S.A.

RANKS – Groups of pipes for various families of voices.

REUBEN SMITH

I'm convinced I could get to interview Mrs Thatcher easier than Reuben Smith of Frome. I certainly got reaction from Chairman David Brown quicker, but he has only got AWD Ltd to run.

The incomparable Reuben is a 'one off' moulded by time and timber, like none other of our breed I've met before. True, his son Bob and grandson Rod are in the business, but this 76 year old keeps his 'hands on the wheel' and calls it 'mucking about'. Missing *Men Mud and Machines* (MMM) I only hooked our elusive entrepreneur after various cancelled dates, as some waggon or trailer demanded his expertise. No words of mine can adequately describe the amazing life of this wiry character.

In 1934 at Witton-le-Wear near Durham, young Reuben had 700 pit sleepers, 6 tons on a 3 ton Vulcan lorry. "I did half an hour in twenty minutes, speeding down a hill, missed the bend, rolled her twice, landing upside down". When he crawled from the wreckage, an onlooker said 'this is a miracle'. However the lad was more annoyed than thankful, his tea bottle was broken, and the written off Vulcan was of less consequence! Next came a six wheeled Ford, with wooden pole attached to the Vulcan's salvaged back axle. This required an H.G.V. test, and licence price of one shilling (it wasn't always £42). Being able to turn round and gauge 20 m.p.h. were the main requirements. The tester knew about as much as Reuben, who was 21 next day.

The arrival of twin daughters led to his seeking a year's contract, hauling for John Green of Silsden, Yorks. It was a load of elm down south to Kent, which it seemed was way past Doncaster, Reuben's previous idea of 'down south'. Later he was sent to other foreign parts, Somerset, and settled there. The next vehicle was a smart petrol engined International, good for 300 cube on those hills, and capable of 75 m.p.h. unloaded.

At this point in his story Reuben produced an ancient cine projector, last unpacked in 1971. I recorded the commentary that accompanied this 30 minutes of sheer delight. There was no disputing the two Leyland Beavers were loaded to the hilt, on Reuben Smith built trailers. "Never buy what you can build" said the projectionist. Reuben's other son in law, Ivan Chant, was pulling them axle deep in slurry up a hill with a Matador, one waggon chained to the other, in the Dartmouth rain forests. More excitement came on the Dunster estate, Minehead. Loading was via an ex W.D. dry sump 11 litre diesel AEC armoured car, that started with ether, at five bob a bottle from the chemist. This vehicle, that once chased

Rommel across the western desert, was now in Reuben's army, chasing timber across the West Country. Crane maker 'Smith' replaced the turret with a 21 foot jib that lowered and protruded 10 feet out front when travelling. Ask the bus company. It penetrated a double decker one day!

Reuben took power from the main gearbox shaft for a Garwood winch that lifted 150 cube. Between jobs, she motored at 60 m.p.h., according to the police, who felt roundabouts were for driving round, not straight over. "Two or three smashed traffic bollards started it", muttered R. "Now this job in Cornwall lasted seven years. "There's the low loader I made." "This is the F.W.D. I shoved a Leyland 600 engine in." "That Matador has an all steel cab, AEC's own won't take a lot. "Yes it's a big tree, but it had more holes than a lace curtain!" The commentary continued. "Here comes our Josephine. She was about fifteen then." At this point a big crawler emerges with a fair load. It's obvious the young lady knew her stuff, as she wended round the stumps. A much younger Reuben was humping fifty yards or so of rope up a sheer bank. The film ends with a bonneted Scammell Highwayman ascending a hill, with trees right out over the pins. "That's how I like to see 'em" said the owner. The film had said it all. Reuben couldn't get the pins out of a new Automower pole waggon, and ended up hiring cutting gear. From then on he designed and made his own bolster fitting and quick release pin, an instant success. The system held when in the Blackwall tunnel with forty footers on, he jammed against another Artic on a bend. "What could I do? I'd been pinched for taking over 30 foot (the limit) over Tower Bridge, but then we have had 35 foot between the bolsters and a 30 foot overhang. That's why I had a permanent 'brickie' rebuilding the wall outside Frome station."

As for Ivan, he left the road with a loaded Beaver, and took down 50 yards of iron railings. Then he hit a tree head on. It was outside Dorchester one night, his lights had suddenly failed. Another time Ivan went into a pub without leaving the Leyland cab! The brakes had failed on a hill, according to a press cutting. He entered the 'Jolliffe Arms' at Kilmersdon, drove through the lounge and out the other side. Rolled the unit in the garden and off loaded the trees in the bar - and still walked away! Now disenchanted with timber haulage, Ivan started a recovery business, preferring to clear up accidents rather than be in them. His pride and joy is a massive USA built Autocar, eight wheeled, twin steer, 350 hp Cummins wrecker, that minusculed their AEC Militant his wife Shirley already thought colossal.

Reuben's other twin daughter Rosa married a young farmer, John Pearce. In no time John acquired a Dodge pole waggon with a Perkins R6 engine. He went to Chichester for a few months in a van, and stayed 12 years, buying a house. The run was from Goodwood to High Wycombe daily. His Leyland Beaver tractor, cheap to buy and run, was an ex BRS box van which Reuben had showed him how to shorten. Hard work, and family support from Rosa and sons John, James and Joe, led to new Scammells, with patent rubber suspension trailer. Later, hauled by a new ERF Cummins 250 in 1976, the vehicle that sold him on the idea of a Jake brake, now fitted to his fleet of Block haulage vehicles. A 'Hough' International Loader shared the lifting with a Matador, that had many refinements. He loaded and hauled gigantic trees from Barnsley park, Cirencester, some up to 9 feet in diameter. The Master had trained the Student well.

Behind the dynamic Reuben is wife Laura who bore him two sets of twins and traipsed from Durham to Devon with the unique Smith conception of logging. Old Reuben is still in timber. It's Scanias that carry the Smith name today. The man who once flew his own plane home because it was cheaper than bed and breakfast, now enjoys yachting and the like.

He left me with this thought: in this life you make up your mind, then go for it. What a character!

__Derby Day 1939__
Reuben and Laura's
twin daughters,
Rosa and Shirley.

__Derby Day (almost) 1989__
Reuben and Laura (centre)
gather Rosa and John (left),
and Shirley and Ivan (right)
around Ivan's colossal
'Autocar'.

4   *Reuben's son Bob at 8 years was capable and safe on this Fowler FD3.*

The broken skid resulted in Reuben winning a bet when he loaded this big tree with shear legs in 10 minutes. Note his home made heavy duty ex-Scammell trailer back end.

Ivan's life was in fact saved by the standing tree. The turntable breaking sent his load past the cab instead of into it.

Reuben's armoured crane, good for 60 m.p.h. according to the West Country Police, who often pursued it.

A typical Smith load in Shepherd's yard, Chilcompton.

Three of Reuben's Scanias and Smith adapted trailers on a Taunton lay-by, early 1980s.

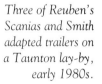

John Pearce's first
vehicle, a Perkins
R6 engined Dodge,
in Sussex where it
all began.

The ex BRS
Leyland box van
John shortened.
The back end is
Foden minus the
diffs. Here well
loaded and bound
for High Wycombe
in 1965.

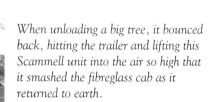

When unloading a big tree, it bounced
back, hitting the trailer and lifting this
Scammell unit into the air so high that
it smashed the fibreglass cab as it
returned to earth.

Barnsley Park, Cirencester. About 900 cube of elm here, two of 'Yorkley Timber' Matadors help John lift and roll load. His 'Hough' loader waits to steady the tree. No margin for error here, all three drivers had to lift in unison, or this new ERF would have been written off in a moment. John's doorless Matador had an air operated hand brake and air leak, causing it to wander off as pressure dropped. Once she crossed a main road and stopped beside a cottage.

Loaded and bound for Yorkshire.

8 *Bert Imbert of Sherrington, Wilts. His ex RAF Crossley does a vertical take off. You should have seen the tree he was pulling!*

EUU 416. Edward Ford of Timsbury and mate Eddie Harris were on pit prop cart with this 6 wheeled Albion when these two lads on the right thumbed a lift to Wareham in 1938. This was agreed, providing the lads helped load up.

FREDA AND JIM

William Walker of Longwick, Bucks was killed in a road accident in 1955. Overnight his 35 year old daugher and secretary, Freda, and son James aged 20, were suddenly responsible for everything.

A sawmill, transport, and 20 Employees, in an active business that started in 1820, "when coffins were 7 shillings each". Freda and Jim got through the next few nightmare years, thanks to the old foreman, Bert Pope, who eased the formidable burdens that bedevilled the young pair.

Neither National Service nor being in the R.A.F. could help Jim now. In fact he had resented rising daily to start up the big McLaren engine and alternator, that powered the mill, from 7 a.m. This was a come down from being an Officer. Radar expertise was useless to a lad who had never bought, felled, or hauled a tree.

That these two young people ran the mill until 1970, is a most notable achievement indeed.

Fred Webb and Bert Jones with one of the three Latils Walkers had new in one year, as the Latil Company claimed in their national advertising.

Fred Webb comes off a wet field with wheeled cleats for extra traction.

A close up of some of the men who made timber history around Buckinghamshire and beyond. Late 1920s.

Driver Fred Bowler gave me this photograph. The New Producer Gas Latil was being demonstrated. Latil designed an engine suitable for charcoal or anthracite burning. It was a fair substitute, but lacked the guts of the petrol engine.

THE STEMPS OF CRANLEIGH

Grandad Stemp was a farmer who found a bit of ground and money for his two boys and son in law to start up in timber and threshing. In due course Stemp Bros., of Cranleigh, Surrey, operated five sets of haulage tackle with 8 men, horses, four steam tractors, and the most glorious assortment of vehicles I've come across. Doug Stemp was a 'Bevin Boy'. Other than those years, it's been timber all the way.

In 1928 his Father created a stir by buying the very latest Caterpillar 30 from 'Tractor Traders' of London - a machine that immediately replaced 25 horses at a stroke. A local blacksmith built a fine pole trailer. The engine was petrol T.V.O., but converted to continuous petrol when its fumes in the woods caused an illness. Later he had a unique 'Caterpillar Diesel 40" 3 cylinder, donkey engine start, with friction drive winch. Three Latils, that ran so long and hot they required decoking every five weeks, were forerunners to two Unipowers. A 'Forester' and a 'Hannibal' WPE 795 their first (and mine), and she's still around today in Suffolk.

At 54 years, Doug's father was pulling a rope across a gulley, collapsed with a heart problem, and never did any hard work again.

Later four AECs joined the fleet, an 'F' Reg. semi-automatic 'Beaver' did well. The other three were a pain, and the last, a 'Lynx' nearly drove Doug mad with problems. In despair, he turned to M.A.N. - a well known German make of lorry. The new 'N' reg tractor has given years of superb service. Simplicity in maintenance is a big attraction. As for mileage, they have lost count of Tacho head replacements. The drivers were long stayers, one nearly 50 years.

Today Doug and his son Brian soldier on in a diminishing market, at least it was until the hurricane of October 1987. That night Doug and his wife had been up late booking, slept heavily, and awoke to find their beloved summer house reduced to match wood beside a wall. The chaos in clearing up during the next few days was aggravated in not knowing who to invoice for what, until the Council took over!

Timber is so great a part of the Stemps' life that even these photographic gems come from the family album. Snapshots of 'Paddling at Clacton, or a 21st Birthday Party, fit naturally beside sister Anne with a Ford V8. This family really loves and lives timber, in spite of the 'Lynx' with a 'Jinx'!

'King of the Road' in 1930.
This little Burrell has not survived, but sister 'Tinkerbell', formally 'The Cranleigh Belle' has.

The new Caterpillar TVO 30 in 1928 that made 25 horses redundant.

One of the first
Caterpillar 40
3 cylinder diesel
with friction drive
winch.

Doug and his sister
with the CAT 40

This new Thorneycroft artic adaptation was
not a success, the trees broke up the body
platform when unloading.

14

A Ford Thames
with a fair load of
sweet chestnut.

The Stemp
children featured
on many timber
snapshots

A top heavy load of
veneer butts on this
Commer two stroke,
noisy, fast and powerful.
"Worn out only after
miles of service"
Doug says.

WPE 795
Unipower
'Hannibal',
new to Stemps
in 1955,
second hand to
me and named
'Eunice'.

A 'Forester' assists
the 'Hannibal' with
a 550 cube elm at
Windsor.

Binding on a
loaded Dodge.

Doug only just managed to load this 800 cube sweet chestnut single handed in Cowdray Park, Sussex.

Doug with the N registered new M.A.N. – still giving valiant service in the 1990s.

A MAN AND HIS MULE

Jack Sanders (no relation) of Aley Green near Luton came up with something new in ex W.D. adaptation. His memories begin with being sent hauling with a World War One ex Army mule when he was aged about twelve. When it would go there was no holding it, when it wouldn't there was no moving it! On one such occasion a passing horse team hooked onto this reluctant moke, dragging it, load and all, changing both its stubborn mood and mind. Jack and brother William worked with their father, William N Sanders, in a unique Luton Coach Building business embracing every operation from felling to fixing hand painted number plates. Father bought a 'Foster' traction engine in King's Lynn and the vendor agreed to acquaint Jack, who was new to steam, how to drive it home.

First Dad wrote on a card that he would honour all debts incurred, which was just as well, since many people had to say "That will do nicely" as the proposed three day trip took a week. The engine had stood ten years and one joint after another failed.

Fortunately, East Anglia is mostly flat, but a passing cyclist on a steep hill near home spotted Jack's problem, jumped aboard, putting the 'Foster' in bottom gear to his surprise. Back at the yard, the knowledgeable stranger was offered a job, and became the driver. Jack's favourite was an ex W.D. chain drive Commer, price seven pounds ten shillings from a Breaker's Yard. Bolsters, seat, and a crude hand winch were fitted to the cab-less chassis.

"We bought 300 oak trees at Folly Farm near Caddington for three pounds apiece. She brought them home, and gave years of service", Jack enthused. Other ex W.D. bargains included a 6 x 4 Morris Commercial and a 1 ton Morris that only cost £4.10s.

A secondhand Fordson Industrial Tractor in 1930 brought in massive loads on a Sanders built (ex lorry chassis) trailer. "Didn't the smooth solid tyres slip on the hills?" I questioned. "Not after I filled the wheels with concrete", replied Jack.

Sadly this remarkable little family was never the same after September 1939. I read the Coroner's inquest report on William Nichols Sanders aged 65. Every gory detail told how Jack had discovered the headless body in the most horrific saw accident ever.

Looking to the future, Grandson Ken showed me the Marshall tractor that is slowly coming back to life. He and his wife Eunice had seen it rotting away whilst on holiday. A 'for sale' notice on it was someone's joke, but the farmer agreed to sell anyway.

From what I see of Ken's re-build, the Sanders claim to "Fine Motor Body Renovations" circa 1920's is still alive in 1989.

This late 1920s Industrial Fordson had no winch, yet fair sized trees were loaded by driving forward with the loading chains, thanks to concrete ballasted wheels.

The trailer was made from an old lorry chassis with a sliding middle bolster for short lengths. Braking was via a lever reached across the draw bar.

When off the road the Fordson was kept busy on belt work in the mill.

For Barn engine buffs, other sources of power were a 10 hp 'Hornsby' bought cheap in the Luton Hatters strike in 1926, and a big 20 hp Blackstone – as seen here.

T.T. BOUGHTON
OF AMERSHAM COMMON

There was a heavy fall of snow in April, 1950 when I commenced at T.T. Boughton and Sons of Amersham, Bucks. My first job was snow ploughing with one of the nine Foden S.T.G. 5 timber tractors. As relief driver I was to become acquainted with many of these, and the two ex W.D. P6 engined Chevs., with Latil winches.

Thanks to the Army's Albion CX 245, 6 x 4 petrol engined 20 ton (later de-rated) flop (as we found) of a tank transporter, there was a great surplus of their excellent artic trailers. Boughtons purchased great numbers of the tandem rear bogies which Trafford Boughton designed, and Denis Stacey, a brilliant welder, built into what became the best balanced and braked timber waggon bar none. Like blacksmith Albert Lock's 'C' hooks, you couldn't fault them.

I received a telegram one Saturday. "Report 6 a.m. for one week". My chance to shine in the daunting West Country (a kind of Timberman's 'Krypton Factor') had come at last. Somewhat disheartened I saw the Devon convoy, who were to have guided me down, leave the yard. My destination was Bishops Lydeard, Taunton. My steed, the odd-ball of the fleet, was a 5 LW engined AEC artic., the 'Lyons Tea Waggon', good for about 400 cube, and so called because of the illuminated cab name-board, and 'Cadby Hall' that showed through the Boughton paintwork at times. An all night brake re-lining was just being completed, and I left two hours late, finding Taunton a long way past Reading, the nearest I had ever been to Somerset. It was dusk when I found this nightmare of sites. I looked for John Dickens in manager's collar, tie, and Landrover. He greeted me in red mud-stained attire, and a D 4. When it was apparent I'd not driven an artic before he just dragged the 'L.T.W.' in backwards, and loaded her.

They were chocolate coloured coated logs that looked like larger versions of the cake roll. Tired and bewildered, I fixed my tail light. John pulled me out, and I headed for Bridgewater and Woods Cafe for a wash, meal and snooze, before trying to make up time up the A38, destination Derbyshire. Half asleep, I went astray in Lichfield and broke a lot of paving in my pathetic attempts to turn round. Although the second trip on Thursday went better, I was a day overdue back at Amersham, about 800 miles later and wiser. It was Saturday night. I was knackered, void of all challenge, and feeling very much a dwarf among giants!

Apart from war service John Dickens, 51 years with Boughtons, started in 1934. In 1937 eight steamers were still at work in this exceptional company that started timber hauling in 1898. Various steam lorries were shortened and fitted with winches, including the famous Foden Speed 6 capable of over 40 m.p.h. Proud driver Alf Hearn would travel to Birmingham and return in a day.

The firm's West of England operation opened up at Wilmington, Devon in 1938, newly married John being sent down to take charge in 1949. I imagine the ensuing six years were anything but an idyllic prelude to the Ruby Wedding Peggy and John celebrated in 1989. From Penzance to Poole, from the Mendips to Mousehole, everything 'Boughton' was this young man's responsibility. His jobs included overseeing local labour, being stand-in driver, fuelling, servicing, and repairing a fleet of extraction tractors that grew from one Fordson and Pole Trailer, to about 12 wheeled and crawler winches.

Boughton's connections with County Tractors accounted for several of this marque - a TD.14, a few Cat D4s and 2 D6, at various times. Therefore, it was: "Call John Dickens" when anything broke, stuck, siezed, blew up or out. Ninety per cent of repairs were done on location. Mud was dug out to drop sumps; a new piston for the Matador fitted near Exeter; a set of 5 L.W. bearings replaced in Wincanton, etc. John's younger brother, Peter, would leave the comforts of his workshop at Amersham to lay bashing some reluctant track in the Devon rains of the 1950s.

A rare breed of drivers operated on a number of sites, that have to be among the worst in the history of U.K. timber extraction and haulage. Names like Daniel Williamson, the Georges - Ginger and Fern - spring to mind, whose skills with the winch knew no limits. One man, who became a legend was known as 'Trigger Bill' (don't ask me why). Trigger's presence on a job was a measure of its severity. Only this doyen loaded an artic in pitch darkness, in the light of a fire he lit by the pole. Only Trigger got away with leaving his D6 overnight in a gentle river to wash the tracks, when flash floods submerged it to within the top six inches of the exhaust. Only Trigger loaded Stan Sear's AEC well back, then cadged a lift for his Cat D2, putting it up crossways behind the cab, between the butts. When his D6 became a hesitant starter, he parked her way up on a log pile, head down, for a roll start. When John and Trigger could find no access to trees felled down a ravine-like bank, Trigger, who had no blade to dig in, cab or roll bar, or tree to rope down from, settled for reverse, and went down like only he would, very fast indeed.

At Monksilver, the TD.14 and D6 jointly roped out 150 cube trees entirely submerged in red slurry. Finally, one of the firm's ploughing engines was brought down. She 'shifted 'em'! Two or three ERF artics trunked this timber up to Essex. The relief drivers would go down to Zeals Cafe, Mere, on the A.303 in a Ford 8, in which the others returned to Amersham.

At South Perrot, things were worse in a 990 acre wood, where pole waggons were loaded bolster deep in this thick clay of the west, most of which dried or dropped off before arrival at Park Royal Timber. I went there but twice, and can assure you artics really were up to their headlights in mud. Over at Timberscombe the ground dropped away so steep the tree tops levelled with the road, and three crawlers brought the butts up to a narrow ledge to load. George Fern and Trigger Bill were free rolling their tractors back down hill. George Ginger just touched his D4 brakes, ripping the tracks and frame off the tractor, as she reared up. What Trigger was in the woods, Jasper (Frank Beaumont) was on the road. He roamed the west with T.T.B's only Matador, recovering and hauling, where others feared to go! Another ex T.T.B. man, Albert Sear, has memories of roping Bert Stratford's loaded ERF round a hillside track, when it overturned. Bert, drenched in engine oil, was freed. The unit was righted, reloaded, and replenished with fuel and oil. The indefatigable Bert drove back to Amersham, minus the cab top and windscreens, still bathed in Gardner skin lotion!

Come the 1960s, John Dickens managed the 20 T.T.B. Haulage Vehicles that transported concrete motorway bridge beams, weighing up to 60 tons, some 90 feet long.

I'm sure these indivisible loads had their own special sets of problems, but after years of wielding spanners in an often far from glorious Devon, I imagine John took them in his stride.

When steam finished, John Boughton still had about 30 sets of threshing tackle, with tractors and winches that left much to be desired. This problem was overcome with a winch designed by his brother, Trafford, the first of thousands of winches that, with other equipment, sell across the world today.

Their father, Thomas Boughton, built a most successful business on Christian principles, hard work, and integrity. Herein is the acorn of the mighty 'Boughton Oak'.

KX 5003 circa 1936, one of six Foden steam waggons converted into tractors by Trafford Boughton. The winch was driven by a 'Munford' launch engine. Extra water tanks and coal bunkers increased the range. This location is Windsor, where double shift drivers changed over on a long haul from Portsmouth to Boxmoor.

Tall John Dickens and younger brother join the Brightman twins, centre, with Dickie Groom. This was Sid's first ERF, HPP 986, with an early BTC 4 in line trailer that would go up on two wheels when cornering and only recover by fierce swerving of the tractor unit, quite a problem in traffic.

A steep pull.

This ex Claridge Leyland was always in trouble. Dick Mounce is roping it out with one of the many County tractors.

Jasper's Matador fitted with a Boughton winch which completely enhanced this tractor.

A few of the nine Foden STG 5 tractors lined up at the Amersham yard.

Almost too late I traced John, the other legendary Brightman twin. A lorry pulled out in front of brother Sid driving the artic – he stopped, but FFJ 849 didn't. Somehow it had missed the end of the pole and John backed off unharmed and they both proceeded on their way.

FFJ 849 when re-cabbed. John drove this Foden for years.

This 30 ton boiler still lined with fire bricks was loaded with double snatch blocks at Berkhampsted brickworks in 1945. The two mile journey to George Evans' scrapyard took an hour in bottom booster gear. Described by John as a nice little Saturday morning job.

Two famous Boughton Fodens, Sid had a 1,000 cube of sawn bulks on his artic here.

The occasion justifies this poor snapshot, here John and Sid's Fodens are transporting sixty ton sections, 90 feet long, from Edgware to the new Westway flyover. Inseperable twins to the end.

THE RUNAWAY KITCHEN MAID

When Lord Minto's son fell in love with a kitchen maid in the last century, he sacrificed all his privileges of birth and became a humble woodman at Burnofield, Northumberland. This romance was to mould the destiny of five generations.

About 1917, tree feller Richard Minto, became a Saw Mill foreman in nearby Netherwitton. The outfit contained a Ransom twin cylinder engine, rackbench saw, and a couple of horses. The family abode was a caravan. Once a month Mrs Minto left this desolate spot, and via pony and trap, and train, went off for provisions. When the wood was worked out, somehow this thrifty woman's saving, and bit of 'Co-op Divi', bought the equipment. Richard found a parcel of timber at Kirkley, near Ponteland, and moved down in 1922. The engine, saw, van, and horses, was now the extent of their belongings. A grubby photograph depicts the engine billowing smoke over the van on the very spot Kirkley sawmills stands today. The Timber Trade Journal records this man rose to become president of the Northern Timber Merchants' Association in 1936. His grandfather had run away, aged 10, to join the trade, and served it 61 years.

Richard had four sons. Of these today, Norman owns Sparkford Sawmill, Somerset, and Ben owns Kirkley. A man named Mr Findley served 45 years from Clerk to Director. In fact, I've never come across so many long serving folk in one firm. The first Fordson managed only 4 m.p.h. on spade lugs. Then industrial models were bought, less their wheels, and rolled along at 25 m.p.h. on big 'Minto designed' ones. Richard's first lorry was an ex tanker Leyland on solid tyres. By 1932, and again in 1936, he had new Leylands. During the war a Ministry ERF Artic and International TD6 Crawler came along.

On a 3-year job near Newbury, Berks, a railway crane lifted 'the pole' as well as the load. Ben felled a larch, and two of them spent all weekend adzeing a new pole into shape, to run on Monday morning.

Much 'Minto magic' was worked on ex W.D. equipment. Two service vans were really Humber Estate Staff Cars, transplanted with Ford 'D' engines, and Leyland transfer boxes, reversed to give over-drive, and 50 miles to the gallon. The masterpiece was a Mack 6 x 6, on which Kirkley brains and brawn mounted a Jones Super 20 full slewing crane. (The War Office had 12 of these cranes, new and unused at Hull, on standby for 'D' Day.) This brought the unit up to 18 tons. From Ruddington came a big step frame trailer for his Crawler, and Janker (logging 'Arch' if you live south of the Pennines), which the Jones would lift onto the turntable. This added another 20 odd tons to the outfit that travelled far and near on an agricultural £5 licence, for 11 years. The police followed it back to the yard when a number plate fell off, not having seen a farm tractor and trailer like this before! On the road Ben would drop the canvas cab top to lower the jib (10 feet out from the Mack bumper). In the woods, flat batteries were overcome with Ben standing on the bumper. He would kick down the handle 3 times on full choke, switch on, and she would fire up on the next kick, whatever the weather.

In the yard, 10 year old Anne was a dab hand with the Jones and, trusted by Dad, lifted building materials. Today she is in the office with husband Tom, not unloading the Volvos!

Of two other Kirkley conversions, one is an Atlas 5000 loader, mounted on a 6 wheeled AEC ex workshop waggon from Aldermaston. Ben replaced the petrol engine with a 7.7 diesel. Still also at work is one of 6 AEC 11.3 engined 4 x 4 Mandators built for Sweden and cancelled, due to currency problems. Ben saw it in chassis form at the Motor Show. AEC fitted a Park Royal Cab. Ben fitted a Unipower winch and jib, that will lift 6 tons. Photographs show her loading giant Douglas fir onto Tuncliffe's double-drive Fodens up at Craigside, bound for Cowes in the Isle of Wight. A special order required 60 footers, 800 cube in 3 trees to a waggon. 2,500 cube in 6 trees - fair old sticks by any standards.

In 1968 Ben and his brother attended a demonstration of the first Volvo BM 840 Loader in Devon. Carl Benson of Volvo U.K. listened to the brothers constructive criticism. The loader, which compared with nothing else then, lacked only thing, a winch, for all the usual reasons. Ben's previous acquaintance with Trafford Boughton accounts for all those Boughton winches on this famous loader. The first went to High Wycombe. The Mintos had the next two. Ben's first of many Volvo waggons, an F86, came new in 1969. He had been to Sweden 10 times, at Volvo's expense, which we must presume is for not being Scania or DAF minded! The other half of this over fifty year old team is Lorien Minto, Ben's wife, who is very much behind this success story.

At Sparkford and Kirkley sawmills, we have the culmination of five generations - a monument to thrift, diligence, innovation, and long service to our trade.

Whoever would dream an 'upstairs-downstairs' romance would have led to all this?

The Fordson, the 1932 and 1936 Leylands line up.

A *typical woodland sawmill scene, the engine, rackbench and a rough tree on a Leyland. But most interesting is the traction engine with overwide wheels built for export to Russia, so useful to Richard Minto.*

'The Kirkley Lumberjack'. The ex ministry ERF has a rare load of axe-felled fir. Note the Jones crane in the background.

A picture that says it all, the International TD6 in action

*The Jones Super 20 crane that Ben Minto mounted on a Mack 6 x 6 with jib
lowered for travelling. What an ingenious combination of 'Ruddington' goodies.*

*This is the AEC 4 x 4 Mandator based winch
tractor of remarkable performance.*

*Long jibs mean high loads. The
Mack's insatiable thirst was
quenched from a 40 gallon drum of
petrol suspended by the crane.*

Loading the giant Douglas firs at Craigside called for all the Mandator's 6 ton lifting abilities.

A very smart Atlas loader mounted by Ben on the AEC ex workshop wagon.

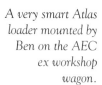

This is the second B M Volvo loader of the hundreds that were to serve our trade.

A stranger carefully selected a rough 20 feet long beech and two limbs in Ben's yard. Two years later this photograph arrived of the 18 foot high figure that now stands in Hexham Abbey. The two limbs (arms) are perfectly mortised into the shoulders.

Lorien and Ben Minto at Kirkley Sawmills

THE BOY WHO LOVED STEAM

Little Geoffrey Gilbert had an inquisitive interest in the steam lorries that delivered materials to his father's builder's yard.

A further fascination was John Sadd's Garrett six wheeled steam tractor that passed his school at Potters Bar, when he was about nine years old. Later the lad wrote off and got maker's details, owner and driver's names.

When father collected timber from Halsey's yard in London Colney, he watched the steam crane with wonder. In his early teens he attached himself to any nearby timber loading operation and got involved on a voluntary basis. He rode miles with pioneers, like Jack Fensom and Jack Cowley. When Gulliver of Enfield was working a rare D.G. Sentinel near Watford, Geoff was there with his camera. Hearing it was for sale, price £15, he was ecstatic! His lack of funds and parents' discouragement, spoilt the dream, but at least he and us can still see this steam winch preserved at Bressingham.

It is of interest that both Geoff Gilbert, and friend George Fensom, remember seeing an ex World War One 1923 4 x 4 Thorneycroft Hathi (the Hindustani for Elephant), winching in 1944. Its vast engine had twin starting handles offset, and chain driven to a central dog that indicates the 'turn-over' power required. Owner Bob Bugg was on contract to George's father.

That boyhood hobby has grown into one of the most comprehensive collections of steam vehicle photographs.

Geoffrey Gilbert is known to many of you as Editor of the journal of the 'Road Locomotive Society'.

Long before my books he captured and brought to life the famous Francis Grover story.

Reproducing these photographs is, for me, an honour.

A boy's devoted hobby has become a heritage. His treasures of yesterday are our heirlooms of tomorrow.

John Sadd's 1932 Garrett 6 wheeled steam tractor and well loaded trailer between Kettering and Malden. Staff left to right are driver Arthur Pipe, Garrett's erecting shop foreman, and Charles Sadd.

J. and G. Halsey of London Colney roping a load together in Ashridge Park, Herts. with their double geared Super Sentinel.

The Sentinel heads for home with a good and long load.

34

Nothing is known of this photograph but what a splendid picture.

Francis Grover ropes out a 325 cube oak in Windsor Park as a Tasker 'Little Giant' holds the Foden.

This Grover Foden ran away and overturned in Bell Lane, Amersham. Her driver was scalded to death. Francis H. Grover ran three sets of tackle and later went on to Latils. In fact he is the only man I know who possessed a watch inscribed by that company. These photographs are by courtesy of the Geoff Gilbert collection.

HENRY THE SHOE BOX MAKER

About 200 superb Oaks from some thirty landowners were donated, as well as much of the transportation, after the devastating roof fire at York Minster in July, 1984.

Finding and milling the required 40 foot long oaks of suitable girth and quality, some valued in excess of £500 was no simple task.

Henry Venables Limited of Stafford, English hardwood specialists for over 125 years, were the obvious choice to co-ordinate this massive task. Almost 700 cubic feet of prime sawn timber, of which part went into the roof, and part the vault, concerned this operation.

Born in 1827, Henry Venables, aged 9 years, became an errand lad to a tallow chandler, and remembered seeing the first train from Birmingham to Manchester. After an apprenticeship he became a carpenter and builder. He had a contempt for book-keeping, and kept it all in his head until it became too much. When the odd tree had to be taken in payment, these were pit sawed back at the yard. During an export boom of shoes for Australia, Henry landed the job to make the thousands of packing cases. These boxes were of the usual Venables standard and appeared like small travelling trunks. After tea each night, his four boys would nail, and Mother lined the boxes with flowered paper. In fact, so attractive were these boxes that they sold readily as Travelling Trunks across Australia.

The Venables name now brought big customers like the Railways and Manchester Ship Canal Company. Large orders were executed from the latest saws. He rose at 5 a.m. (even weeks before his death at 85), opened the Mill at 6 a.m., then walked miles, buying timber and visiting the fallers. He could walk 20 miles a day at 70. The fortunes of the Company are based on a large purchase of prime oak, on which their great name for dry oak was built. The 17 acre site today, where the first building covered Henry's pit saw, is now the scene of one of the trade's largest and most modern kiln-drying plants for over 6,000 cubic foot of timber, backed up by the latest in automatic log sawing machinery. The Company can boast a unique technical service to architects and specifiers alike. Apart from standard joinery etc, timbers for restoration of all period buildings is available. 'One off' orders, from Church Pews to modern Bank Fittings, are part of their timber engineering service.

Henry Venables Limited remain a standard of comparison in the trade, as one would expect from a Founder, who made throwaway packing cases so well they became a saleable product far across the world.

A superb oak is being towed out by this large USA-built 'Holt' tractor.

I understand this is a Sentinel-built 6 wheeled timber carriage.

This load featured in Foden advertising in the 1930s.

Axe-felled trees being loaded by a Foden.

Roping out – these five photographs are magnificent. Sent by Geoffery Venables from the firm's archives. They were simply all captioned "Bagots Park" 1932.

A load of ash veneer logs bound for Europe direct are being loaded here by Bill Ewin's Magirus Deutz and Highland Bear Loader.

BIG FOOT OF BRENCHLEY

I have come across quite a few AEC 'Militants' in timber, but unlike baby sister the 'Matador', most have been pensioned off by now. Therefore, how refreshing to hear of born-again Militants in 1989. It's the brain child of a couple of likely lads, currently in timber - Peter Cornish and Paul Churcher.

Peter Cornish of Brenchley is a well-known Kent timber merchant. His story starts with helping Dad fell pulp wood before leaving school. A Fordson Major Trailer and Ford D1000 lorry were his first kit. Fifteen years on, his turnover is £1$^{1}/_{2}$ million as he shifts 2,000 tons of mixed timber a week. His fleet of mostly Scania and ERF waggons are well-known across Kent and Sussex.

Paul Churcher is an all-rounder, from planting mature trees, felling, saw doctoring, and fitting, but most of all he is into fabrication and welding. By a quirk of fate, due to the effect of the coal strike on mining timber in 1985, these two men met up. The concept of the 'Militant' conversion to an ultra modern forest machine was born of these two minds. A timber merchant, John Drake, had the idea first, but Peter and Paul were bursting with their own futuristic plans. This was no 'weekend weld-up'. There was much more to our 'Thoroughly Modern Millie', a great deal indeed. 'Big Foot' as 7 year old Aaron Cornish called the first one, needed her axles widening to take the giant 23.1 x 26 tyres she rides anywhere on, and beams replace springs. On the fourth, and latest model MK4, all functions are electronic, including steering, and the swivel seat that enables forward or reverse driving, whilst using the Hiab 070 crane. The cab has all-round vision through bullet proof glass, sound proofing, sun roof, and stereo radio cassette facility. Doubtless a cocktail cabinet would be extra! Did timber carters ever have it so good, I ask? The 'Millie' had proved the perfect base machine. That well tried AEC 11.3 engine turned those big wheels up to 55 m.p.h. on test. Loads of 20 tons are no problem. Reliability and profitability are assured at a most modest cost, compared with a new forward tree harvester. It was in the wake of the 1987 hurricane these machines really proved themselves. Day after day one man and a 'Millie' extracted from 60 to 100 tons a day. How I would have loved to have accepted Paul's invitation to go down and try out Big Foot, but that was not to be.

The ingenious adaptation of weapons of two world wars by our men of timber never ceases to amaze me. These resourceful men are yet again proof of a breed of innovators that belongs to our trade alone. AEC Southall would have been proud of 'Big Foot'.

There have been many adaptations of the 6 x 6 AEC Militant, but nothing quite like this before.

Peter Cornish, left, and Paul Churcher with their joint brainchild 'Big Foot' Mark 3

With all their refinements, these enterprising machines costs are far lower than their new counterparts. This is Big Foot Mark 4.

ROYAL PARKS
AND ROYAL TREES

In 1988, for Tom Stanley, life was ebbing away, but he intended to ride in the Volvo eight wheeler then on order, and clung on with all the tenacity he had shown for eighty years in timber. It seemed his wish was not to be, and I was invited to give a word of tribute at his funeral in April, 1988. Outside the Church, the characteristic smell of a new vehicle prevailed -the hearse had been replaced by the gleaming new FL.10. Tom's last wish was to be her first job. Dave Shirley, of Dawson Commercials, negotiated Chipping Norton cemetery with the dignity of a Rolls, and another great warrior of wood was laid to rest. £188 worth of flowers were not left to fade and die, rather the family that had founded my fund-raising idea had this amount of donations channelled to CORDA, the Heart charity.

The children, Maureen and Patrick, reminisced about 'The Fire Fly', an ex Woodstock Bedford Fire Engine that Tom had converted to a timber lorry. The sale of the pump, brass ware and fittings, just paid for the adaptation. Always 'on the button' thanks to dual ignition, not surprisingly it drove like a Fire Engine as well! The memories were legion, but I was caught out without my tape recorder.

Brian and Pat, Brian and Pat, where have you been?

We've been up to London to see the Queen.

Brian and Pat, Brian and Pat, pray what did you there?

33,000 Cube is an estimate fair.

Surely each royal tree has its own T.P.O? Yes, we've heard, said the lads, but the hurricane didn't know!

I had a Brompton hospital appointment a few days after the great storm in October 1987. Down Park Lane the coach provided a conducted tour of that horrific night's gales, when huge trees that had stood the test of time succumbed to this unmerciful blow. An orchestra of chain saws rose in a crescendo, above the noise of the traffic. Over 800 trees lay in Royal Green and Hyde Park and Kensington Palace Gardens for the Department of Environment to dispose of. Invitations to tender brought no sensible reactions, due to the enormity and problems of such an operation. Probably because of Brian Gorton's reputation (the other name on the FL 10) for timber work on Crown Land, like 'Chequers' for many years, he was persuaded to undertake this thankless job. Brian and Pat sized up the daunting task but by now the trade had fallen overnight, like the trees. Even 18 months on, Pat's was one of 17 waggons at a mill waiting to disgorge his contribution to the biggest timber glut of all time.

Plane and Lime are never in large demand, particularly when infested with in-grown non-ferrous, non-detectable shrapnel 30 feet up. True all timber had been extracted from Buckingham Palace's gardens, but working daily in highly sensitive areas, among the Horse Guards in Rotten Row and the location of the I.R.A. bandsmen bombing, meant high security. Like working in front of Kensington Palace, home of Prince Charles and Princess Diana, where the big red chopper came in and out over the loads. No wonder each vehicle, even the loader, had to display a police permit, with frequent spot checks.

Brian's hand-picked team were Geoff Sullivan of Chesterfield, with his smart Scania 142 M - 420 HP 'Mile Eater' and triaxle trailer. Basil Hyde, of High Wycombe, and his faithful from new 'T' Reg ERF, now replaced with another nag from the same stable. His son, Mitchell, had a Renault 260. Pat's FL 10 ran between his loading the others with 'Big Allis', his ex Army loader. First Brian spent two weeks measuring and sawing the logs, as did Pat, collecting and stock piling the timber that covered acres.

Three inches of rain fell overnight before the start in May, 1988. Flooded under-passes awaited the waggons as they left with the first loads from Constitution Hill beside the Palace, all bound for the Midlands. They were long 12 hour days. London Plane is hard and dense to cut, and as heavy as Beech to haul. Loads included various rare species of trees that had neither been sawn nor milled before. Tourists, souvenir hunters, wood turners, took more unexpected time. As for the waggons, they had to be loaded about right. Once through those park gates they were in the thick of London's worst traffic for half an hour or so. 33,000 cube was hauled in over 60 loads on time, in this most demanding, unusual operation. Every vehicle must have earned the right to display the 'Royal Coat of Arms' which will not be forthcoming.

At least the Department of Environment was pleased, and that alone is surely praise indeed.

Tom's last wish was the Volvo's first job.

44 *Mitchel Hyde with his Renault 260 waits as Pat loads Basil's T reg. ERF beside Park Lane.*

The old Albert Memorial is the background for the new Volvo FL10 320 with a 26 ton 'T' ride back axle and a few other inbuilt goodies. Loading is via a Hiab 900.

The 1902 bronze 'Physical Energy Monument' – Pat gives a modern interpretation with his 'Big Allis'.

*Pat and Geoff survey
the Serpentine moments
before the Scania leaves
at 7 a.m.*

*Pat watches in
Kensington Palace as
(C and D's) big red
chopper takes off.*

*Geoff's Scania being
loaded in Rotten Row
midst the Horseguards.*

*Pat with the FL10 and
a typical Stanley
maximum load.*

BIG MEN, BIG LOADS

No Timberman's 'Hall of Fame' would be complete without reference to The Yorkley Timber Company of Ross-on-Wye.

I only ever saw one of their waggons, and he had more beyond his back bolster than I had in front of mine.

During the early 1930s Albert and Howard Porter traded as The Yorkley Coal Company. Then turning to pit props, they progressed into every facet of round timber haulage. During the period 1940-50, a most comprehensive fleet of ex W.D. heavy duty vehicles was built up by the brothers, converted by Nash & Morgan of Whitecroft, Glos. These were operated by a body of dedicated Timbermen, 80 to 90 strong at one time.

There was nothing ex W.D. about the Hippo engined 1930 Leyland Bull. This vehicle, with its draw-bar trailer, was designed to carry 22 tons. However, when later re-engined with a 6 L.W., and converted to an artic pole waggon, it often carried 30 tons. The Bull covered over a million miles in the hands of Albert Porter and the famous Mickey Fricker, an enormous man, whose strength extended to off-loading softwood logs weighing five to seven hundredweight. The Company came to operate several Caterpillars, ex W.D. Dodges, Chevs, Quads, 12 Matadors from a stock of 20, 6 rigid and 6 wheelers, and various lorries. The real heavyweights consisted of an Albion, Scammell, and later ERFs. It is 4, ex W.D. 6 x 4 Foden Artics that shifted some of the biggest regularly recorded loads I have come across.

Les Hodges was with the firm from 1953 until 1984 and describes the seven-hour trips up the A.49 to Ryeden and Anderson of Bolton, where on arrival one weighbridge ticket recorded a loaded Foden at 48 tons. Or 975 cube of Ash up to Oates of Worksop, and a welcome kip on the medical room bed. Burt Powell had exploits too, like taking a Matador from Ross to Okehampton, loading two big artics, and returning the same day. (What a strong left leg he must have had?)

Then there was 'The Tank', the nickname given to an ex W.D. AEC 0856 6 x 6 armoured operational Office and Wireless room, used by Senior Officers under Field Marshall Montgomery in the Western Desert. Cutting the body off reduced some of its 18 tons weight and made room for a turntable, pole, and tandem axle, that corresponded with the war-like cab, that held no fears for swinging trees! When all efforts to drill the armour plate failed, the driving mirrors were welded on. This unique looking vehicle delivered a giant Cedar, 880 cube, in one lump, down to Princes Risborough. The 9.6 engine did just 4 m.p.g. 'The Tank' was never involved in an accident, since her poor braking was overcome by good gear shifting!! She once threw a propshaft, but this was overcome for all time by one from a Diamond 'T'. All loads were required to reverse into Clayton's Sawmill of Birmingham, which was a kind of 'lorry driver of the year' test. I've seen H.G.V. men get paid for doing less on Noel Edmonds Show. To see little Bill Beech reverse 'The Tank' was an event they should have sold tickets for! One moment he would hang out of the offside, then cross the ample cab to view the nearside, as he crept back in super low gear. The long drag up the A49 to the 'Lazy Trout' cafe would be taken at 10 m.p.h. with 800 cube up, as so called heavy waggons flashed past him.

Les Hodges recalled days when even a 7 a.m. arrival at Windsor Park would reveal six others waiting to load before him - days when loads were so high three different bridges were too low on one route.

Alan Porter, Albert's son, dipped into the archives for me.

When 6 m.p.g was considered poor for the Fodens, their gross overloading made performance look good. the Foden 'norm' was 700 to 900 cube of hardwood, often ordered 60 to 75 feet long. Special orders were for the Navy's 'Ark Royal', in 1940 and also 'H.M.S. Victory'.

Yorkley once held the largest supply of Walnut veneer logs in the U.K. In one 1950 sale alone over 100 butts, all 24" quarter girth plus and larger, were sold. Today, the cost alone of security would be astronomical! They were fined many times for failing to maintain minimum speeds within the Mersey Tunnel, but as one driver put it, "Even emerging from the tunnel at 5 m.p.h. with 970 cube wasn't bad going!

Alan relates how in the bad winter of 1962/3 regular customer, Cooper Limited of Sheffield, beseeched them for a load to keep going. Early Monday morning Bill Beech left with a huge load on a snout-nosed Scammell. No word was heard for three days, then he turned up with horrific snow-drift stories. Coopers were so delighted they offered Bill a job until the weather improved but Bill said, "No, my Boss do want I", and left for Ross. When he drew in the yard the following Friday, Albert Porter welcomed him with "I've been thinking of you Bill", to which Bill replied, "I've been thinking of thou too, but thou bist still alive"!

In the snows of 1950 driver Charlie Vincent was sent with a Matador to pull a big tree that threatened a house just outside Ross, then he was to load it on a lorry. Next morning no one could account for a 40ft long, 100 cube Elm that laid in the yard. No one but Charlie, who said, "The lorry never came so I used my initiative and tushed it home". This man had calmly winched the tree half a mile through the centre of Ross-on-Wye! Whether this comes over as resourcefulness or madness is irrelevant. Deep down in these men is an expertise of their breed that knows no limits.

I was not privileged to meet Albert or Howard Porter.

Their acumen for business was obvious. Their gift to win such loyalty from their men, and loads from their machines, must be known only to themselves.

The famous 1930 Leyland 'Bull' that covered well over a million miles. Photographed for the Leyland magazine, in the yard of Skinner and Richards, Liverpool. Mickey Fricker made sure the long load warning was necessary!

Les Hodges with a regulation load on an ERF in the 1970s. Note the ERF's springs are mounted above the axle for greater load clearance.

One of the ex WD double drive Fodens being loaded in adverse conditions. Remember, 900 cube was the norm for these Fodens.

No comment!

Les Hodges being unloaded in Barchards of Hull, their giant fork lift would take the whole load in one bite.

Sadly we have no photographs of little Bill Beech with the armoured 6 x 6 AEC, but this is the 880 cube cedar he took to Princes Risborough with it. Move trees like this, and you are a timber haulier my son!!

THE SOMERSET LUMBER MILL

A wet day in Bournemouth prompted an inland drive in 1986. My wife, Helen, suspected an ulterior motive when we crawled through the village of Tisbury, Wilts. Was my finding an F.W.D. at work too transparent to be a coincidence? Inside the busy little mill Roger Staddon and his sister Margaret, (an ex wartime lumber Jill), held the key to exceptional timber history. Their father, J. J. Staddon, started this business in the 1920s. The Somerset Lumber Mill was formed in 1935, when a large parcel of oak was purchased in Crewkerne as an investment. It was the idea of a friend who had been to America. Where else does 'Lumber' crop up in English timber?

Roger's brothers, John and Gordon, set up home in a cabin and a temporary saw mill that is near Crewkerne to this day.

The Staddons were a family of born innovators and natural timber haulage adaptors. An enormous 1908 Bessmer yacht engine drove the mill. A model 'T' Ford mounted circular saw powered by a bullnose Morris engine served as a super mobile saw. Winching was via a 1926 McCormick-Deering tractor, with home made winch, and 1929 ex W.D. Morris Commercial 6 x 4. An AEC Artic was re-engined with a Chrysler straight 8, and a Karrier 6 x 4 slogged for years; eventually she was re-fitted with a Buick engine and Morris radiator. The list of vehicles and transplants is endless. The Staddons were shrewd buyers at Ministry of Supply sales. A popular purchase was a couple of Dodge 6 x 4 WK 60 (Cab over engine) breakdown gantry waggons, right hand drive, built for the British Army. The winch was by 'Garwood', but the amazing feature of these vehicles was the 'Thornton' two speed double drive. On or off the road, this double reduction was fantastic. One truck was adapted as a bedwaggon, the other as an artic, with a backend made up from a 1930 Foden tanker. Roger and John ran her regularly from Crewkerne to Essex. The Dodges were goers and, if desired, those forty horses would motor at 60 m.p.h.!

F.W.D. are three hallowed letters with the Staddons. Matador is an ugly word hereabouts. Constant four wheel drive, and diff lock gives the edge over AECs, insisted Roger. The two faithful F.W.D. Su-coe, (ex Uncle Sam's Lease Lend) looked good to me. One is re-engined with a 4 L.W., both have Staddon designed jibs, with a tested S.W.L. of five tons, that has lifted 10 tons with the chassis blocked. Continuous use to this day has included snow ploughing yearly from 1949 to 1985. Winter 1962-63 saw both F.W.D.s running by day and by night for weeks on end, relentlessly clearing the roads of Wiltshire.

Tisbury is the home of the famous Parmiter Agricultural Manufacturers, dating from the 1800s, from whom an order for 160 packing cases had just come in, and Margaret and Roger needed to press on. If the words 'Lumber Mill' conjure up big Yankie machines handling huge logs, then the Staddon set-up was most aptly named.

John and sister Margaret Staddon, who was drafted into the Womens Forestry Corps, are seen here winching with a Fordson tractor, near Tisbury during the Second World War.

This pre-war 6 x 4 Karrier gave years of yeoman service. Here she brings a load of ash butts off the Fonthill Estate, nr. Tisbury in W.W.2.

A most remarkable vehicle this, one of the two Dodge WK60 Special COE. Good ground clearance and superb traction made these vehicles ideal for timber work.

Viewed from the rear, we see the ex Foden single axle with above its share of a 425 cube elm.

A long load and a scenic view.

In the woods. These Dodges were purchased with low mileages and proved an ideal investment. Even so, I have not seen this model used in timber elsewhere.

One of the FWDs lifts a biggish tree with ease.

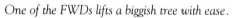

This engine's steering chain broke when steaming flat out at 8 mph. Note the two pulleys on the sturdy Staddon devised jib.

This 15 ton engine pushed the FWD a little down the hills.

Both FWDs snow ploughed yearly from 1949 to 1985 – one FWD was still at work in the yard the day I called in 1986.

MR. UNIMOG

Alec and Pauline Blake live at Fewcott, near Upper Heyford, and all the U.S. Air Force decibels that means. I imagine their ear protectors are for home use, and Alec yearns for the peace of his chainsaw's roar in the woods! Bill Blake, Alec's father, died of cancer when he was 52. Alec, then a 22 year old digger driver, hoped to continue the timber tradition with his younger brother who, regrettably, was killed shortly afterwards in a motor cycle accident. I therefore especially admire this man's array of forestry equipment and courage. Typical of his generation, and like many of his kind, his mainstay is an American-type Skidder. Alec's is an S. Reg. 66B Clarke Ranger 165 h.p. V6 Cummins engined. This has constant 4 W.D., and enough grip and 'poke' to pull a 400 cube hardwood up into its roller box, and tush it out. Alternatively, the Clarke has tongs, with an 8 foot spread. Questioning the economics of the Skidder over here, Alec reminded me, on a clear fell 35 acre site, as big trees were being felled, this machine extracted four to five thousand cube per every four hours. Now that really is shifting timber!

Alec's enthusiasm for his 1985 Unimog was obvious. Everything appears air controlled in the comfy cab. This work-horse pulls a tilting bed low loader that transports his Cat. 941, and the Ranger. A lot of 'Blake design' has gone into the bolster trailer loaded with 450 cube of Corsican fir, that romped along at 40 m.p.h. plus.

Unemployed Albert Friedrich, ex Daimler-Benz Engine Designer, envisaged the idea of a combined field and road tractor in 1946. His Unimog (all purpose motor vehicle) has won acclaim across the world, particularly at Fewcott!

An early 411 Unimog converted by James Jones. Roll bars are not ornamental in the Scottish Highlands!

Alec's latest Unimog 1700, 200 hp, new October 1989. The 412 cube of ash and beech was loaded with the Atlas 3006 crane. A lovely all purpose machine.

The 'Clarke Ranger' excells in these conditions near Milton Keynes.

PETER, DAVE AND IVOR

Ben Hinton, whose fund of knowledge of Midland characters in the timber trade never ceases to amaze me, met and interviewed Peter Holmes and Ivor Condlyffe of Bromsgrove.

Peter had a short, but interesting adventure with an ex U.S. Army Diamond 'T' 6 x 6. It was purchased in 1948 for £350 at a U.S. surplus sale. The tractor unit had a Hercules petrol engine and front mounted winch. The trailer was a 40ft flat bed mounted on a pole waggon and intended for transporting boxed gliders. Bought to haul a parcel of 60 feet long Turkey Oak, the 'D.T.' did well, but on country roads and lanes it was cumbersome and thirsty, a mixed blessing, it was dismantled in 1951. S.T.H. Brooks & Sons of Redditch often hauled into Chambers & Marsh of Oldbury. Peter recalled their huge loads and Ben remembered the glow of their Latil's red hot exhaust manifolds at night. Sam and Don Brooks hauled with horse and steam for their father. Later they operated as Brookes Bros., for ten years, with two new Latils. In 1936 they split up and it then became S.T.H. Brookes & Sons, all *eight* of them!, David being the eldest. By 1970 Sam retired, and the boys took over and ran their own Saw Mill at Hunt End, with three sets of waggons. To support themselves, these eight boys, minus any employees, survived on father's teaching of initiative, and heavy loading. The company ceased when the Mill became a Factory Site in 1980. The vehicles included ERF Ford Transcontinental, 2 Foden two strokes, a D.A.F., and an ex W.D. 6 x 4 Thornycroft. For five years Sam would remove the trailer and turntable from this vehicle, and replace it with the original Army body, for a week's family holiday. Each year he would set off for Wales with his wife and all eleven children, since there were three girls as well as the eight boys.

David Brookes rebuilt Matadors and made pole trailers capable of carrying giant single green elm trees to specialists Alfred Groves. I note cubages like 625, 650, 700, 724 and 898. Work that out at 25 cube to the ton!

Today David builds recovery vehicles and is restoring the 1950 Latil MWP 86. Later owned by Bates Heavy Recovery of Evesham, this unstoppable (as usual) Latil was towed to sites on an 'A' frame and became a most valued wrecker.

About 1941 Sam was in the Birmingham Thornycroft Depot and noticed a most unusual vehicle for sale. It was one of two experimental units built and sent to Finland in 1933. It was a 6 x 4, with 14 x 20 tyres. In Finland it had skis fitted on the front axle and was built to tow two logging trailers. A big diesel tank in the cab fuelled a massive Thornycroft 4

cylinder 11.3 litre engine with 8" diameter pistons. The asking price was £100. Sam got it
for £90.

It appears the 'blow lamp' starting was not a success in sub zero temperatures. Sam matched the 11.3 to a comparable tandem pole trailer and found the unit slow but very powerful. Loads between 600 and 700 cube were no problem to the Thornycroft and in the 1940s she had few rivals. It was sold in 1945 for £12. Sam's proudest moment was when ascending a hill near High Wycombe he came upon three sets of Boughton's tackle nose to tail and loaded. Despite the Thornycroft's load, Sam changed down and passed all three of them!

At 85, Sam Brookes has battled with cancer for some time, but disease, like difficult trees, will not easily overcome this Midland timber haulage history maker.

My previous references to the first known timber operation in the Bible (first book of Kings, Chapter V) leads me to Ivor Condlyffe, near Bromsgrove.

As a Royal Engineer, in charge of a sawmill in Lebanon, Ivor followed in the steps of King Hiram, beside the reputed route. Still labour intensive in World War Two, about 300 men manhandled every load of fir and cedar off, in and out of the mill. An old Renault truck carried the sawn timbers to the Army's own railway siding, where again orders were loaded by hand, destined across the Middle East.

The trees were felled on the mountain face, where one man a week was lost as he followed the tree down! Mules 'tushed' them out for loading in the snow, and R.E. snow dozers kept the pass open. Similarities in transportation end here, since old Hiram had no 6 x 6 'G.M.C.' and 'Studebakers' to zig zag the timber 65 miles of hairpin bends down to the mill, and temperatures of 90 degrees. Out of 32 waggons the aim was to keep 22 on the road. I imagine brake lining abilities would be at a premium in the workshop.

Ivor Condlyffe felled his first Birch pole in 1927. Later, with his brother-in-law and elder brother, Eric, they felled giant silver Fir that topped out at 120 feet, one of which cubed at 844 foot, at Fonthill Abbey. These trees were planted by Bickford, the Slave Trader.

A little Burrell engine that hauled and drove a rackbench was continuously brought to its knees by these young men. Caught pulling hard with a 'spark arrester' that didn't!, they had the police interested in 28 feet of tree out beyond the rear bolster, with no red lamp! When a branch in the woods knocked the chimney off, the lads beat a sheet of corrugated iron into shape, which lasted until this abused little steamer was scrapped for £4.10 shillings.

Ivor recalled the hungry 1930s, and hard times, when a vendor sat over a hole in a fallen tree, until the Buyer bought, and moved on.

In the days before debt collectors, Ivor's brother cycled twenty miles seventy-two times to get £70. There were times when a good engine was left to rust and rot in a wood for the lack of coal money and times when a timberman's skills had to include dodging creditors, as well as falling trees.

The Condlyffes, like their engine, found nothing easy in timber.

With pole and adjustable back end, Peter's Diamond T was ready made for timber, but not in Worcestershire lanes.

Sam Brooke's Thorneycroft whilst on demonstration in Finland, circa 1933. The 11.3 engine appears to be well covered. Photograph courtesy the Arthur Ingram collection.

Dave on the Fordson Major helps Sam with the Latil (now being restored by Dave), roping in nightmare conditions.

*Nightmare
conditions!
Only yards from
the road.*

The Brookes never loaded light – this AEC was starting to get a natural 'Beavertail'.

Dave with their new DAF.

Ivor's brother and brother-in-law with the much used and abused little engine with home made chimney stack. The lad is the photographer's son, who knew how to pose.

Ivor in 1989 with his trusty ex WD Commer 4 x 4, with mid-mounted anchor just visible.

Ben Hinton came up with this fine Foden Artic photograph. Nothing else of this firm is known to us.

Some of us have seen this all before, the miscalculated pull perhaps, wires down, and man with flag. This picture from the Ben Hinton Collection tells all.

KEN AND ROSE OF KINVER

It took a Doctor's letter to get Ken Wrigley released from Stourbridge Grammar School.

Father, John Wrigley, on his death bed, had about six months to enlighten his son in the ways of saw milling and timber. Cancer of the throat did nothing to enhance the vital communications.

Kinver sawmill was powered by a 15 foot diameter water wheel from the Stour, which required a 5.30 a.m. sluice control for a head of water and half a bucket of oil on the bearings. The latter had been Ken's pre-school job long since. Years later a 150 h.p. motor replaced the wheel.

After the funeral in 1928, 15 year old Ken surveyed the yard void of all timber - the business capital had been ploughed fruitlessly into radium treatment on John.

Three men, thrice Ken's age, had to be paid. Wages were met just by Ken sawing and hawking logs at a shilling a bag. The lad assessed his assets. A bicycle, a 7 lbs felling axe, 30 shillings savings, and one hell of a mind determined to survive!

Today a two hour commute to work and back is not unusual, and it was so then with Ken, on his bike, up to 15 miles over the Malvern Hills, felling for 10 hours in between. This was the price of retaining the Mill and by the sweat of his brow he paid for it!

His next dream to come true was to buy a bandsaw that would take three coffin length butts in line, and produce $^3/_4''$ boards, with great precision, a word that epitomises Ken's approach to life.

The firm's war work was cutting Bailey Bridge planks, and ammunition boxes. The three men were automatically exempted, and young Ken was called up, then released. A boy Boss? Not a likely story!

The Darke family of Worcester kept a friendly eye on Ken and slowly prosperity followed perspicacity with plenty of perspiration in between.

Now I bring you to what must be the two most cosseted vehicles in the trade. Bedford YRE 947 chassis cab, new from Lowes of Kinver in 1952. Ken's carpenter built the ash framed body, still in good shape after 37 years of steady deliveries. Now modernised with flashers and stoplights, she sailed through her M.O.T. September 1st, 1989, mileage 52,644. Probably the world's most immaculate Matador, in daily use, is LRF 463B, ex Ruddington in 1964.

Prails of Hereford overhauled the engine and fitted the jib and anchor. She came home and has never been out of the yard since, would you believe. The Kinver sawmill's reputation for quality wood today is in part due to loyal workers and Ken's wife, Rose, who has shared running the business to this day. Ken's father was active in public life, as is his son. In fact, it is noteworthy that both Rose and Ken have given umpteen years of service to two different local councils. As the developers surround the Sawmill and hover like speculative vultures, the Owners are unimpressed. They have grown not to expect easy money. Besides, Ken has just had a new hip. Customers are depending on him. Why on earth should he give up?

They say you can't put old heads on young shoulders - well, John Wrigley did, without choice.

How proud he would have been today.

Ken Wrigley (right) and fellow craftsmen knew how to 'set up' a tree for felling.

86 MUY, AEC Mammoth Major, owned by S. Darke and Sons, with a heavy elm. Felled by Roy Finch near Bewdley in 1972. Rose is on the left and Ken is on the right.

Ken's immaculate Bedford that still sails through her M.O.T.s.

LRF 463B. This has to be the world's most cosseted Matador. With driver Peter Guest (26 years service with Ken and Rose).

THE MAN WHO MADE HORSESHOE NAILS

The first salesman ever to call on me was Ken Haigh of James Jones & Sons, Larbert, Scotland.

From shackles to winches, snatch blocks to simple half track conversions, you name it, they either made it or got it from those that did.

Seeking to honour this company in "Stories of Round Timber Haulage" (SORTH), I wrote to them in 1983. Inadvertently, it went to their foundry division and brought an account of James Jones' development of his patent 'J' horseshow nail in 1850 and their World War One boat building up in Buckie. In fact their constructing of an all wooden cargo ship that carried tons of timber south was the only reference made to timber haulage.

At an early A.P.F. demonstration, the founder's great grandson, Airlie Bruce Jones, and Chief Engineer Bill Baillie, enlightened me. Ever since, I have always called on their stand to wish them a full order book, if not to help do so. We are thinking about a company that employs 360 people in two divisions, timber and engineering. During the last six years this company has invested over £9 million in its timber operations.

James Jones supplied the first telegraph poles to the G.P.O. in 1893. Nearly a hundred years on they deliver over 50,000 creosoted poles per annum. Seven Jones' sawmills are fed in part from 2,500 acres of the company's own forests, so much of which grow on mountainsides battered by wind and rain, the like only Scotland knows. The ultimate testing ground of man and machine, if either are going to crack it, will be here. All J.J. equipment therefore is first sold to themselves, so to speak. Jones pioneered and proved 'Skylines', a method where a lattice tower is erected on a tractor with a double winch and cables. This extracts timber high above the trees from up to 600 metres, 2 tons a time, from gradients where neither horse nor tractor could stand. A chockerman puts his life in the hands of his wincher, as he directs operations via his two-way radio. Not the odd treacherous job this, but a daily way of life for some 70 units working the west coast, Bill tells me. Cables, then hydraulics and forestry engineering were applied to timber in what is now known as Forwarders, Harvesters, Skidders, Loaders, Cranes, and Grapples, embraced in the Jones trade name 'Highland Bear'. I chatted on with the man who has put some of the 'hug' into this bear, worldwide.

Bill Baillie remembers using the baby Ransome crawler for thinnings, where branches were too low for the horse. About 60 Unimogs were fitted with winches, and an effective, if simple, under-belly protection was afforded by lengths of conveyor belting from front to rear, and so on.

Airlie Bruce Jones tells me Bill came to the timber industry in 1948 after war service in the R.A.F. Those were the times when the days of steam were numbered, (although an artic vehicle was not allowed to run at more than 16 miles per hour) and the foundations of the present day timber industry were being laid.

What he brought to the old established family company, James Jones and Sons, where many of the family and employees were second and even third generation brought up in the world of wood, sawdust and steam, was a wide knowledge and experience beyond his years, of the youthful road transport industry and the new-fangled diesel engine that went with it.

There are plenty of problems, when you are dropped into the glaur* well over the top of your boots amongst steam and woodmen, who have seen it all before, and it makes a pretty powerful challenge to a young man. Needless to say Bill Baillie was made of pretty tough stuff. Anybody who at the age of 14 could "gie a haun" to his uncle to change the diff on the top of Shap in winter is unlikely to be beaten easily by the bluster of the old hands. Over the next few years he had to go through an apprenticeship in wood, and dare I say it, his standing began to grow even amongst yesterday's experts. Steam, the universal power source for Jones' mills in the 30s and 40s, gradually changed during the 50s to electricity and diesel, and Bill's background could not have been better suited for these changing times.

Although many of the old boys worked on under Bill in later years, for instance maintaining the dieselised steam cranes in the hardwood mills or shoeing the odd horse still used on thinning work, a new team of "Baillie's men" who served their time in Jones' engineering works at Larbert came to the fore. With a fleet of over 250 vehicles to service the requirements of 33 sawmills, Bill established an invaluable support service for the company's transport operations.

Of all the ex W.D. vehicles under Bill's wing Chevs., Diamond Ts, Guys and Albions won his praise. Ford 4 x 4 were rather a disaster and Bedford Q.L.s were never a success. Of the Latil it was said its engine and winch were more use in another vehicle! (Pause for the author to recover.)

What other Company could boast 21 Matadors during the late 50s and 60s? The standard round wood haulage vehicle for Jones' hardwood and big softwood trade was the Baillie designed AEC Matador, fitted with a swan necked jib crane, with an assortment of local mods, and the Larbert joiners built ash framed cabs for replacements. Those Matadors managed a lot of the extraction, as well as the loading, and haulage over the easier sites, but D2/4s or TD9s, using logging arches made at Jones Buckie Boatyard Engineering shop, worked where the Matador rope couldn't reach.

Running 20+ crawlers, servicing the fleet, and keeping a back-up in re-build state in reserve, gave Bill a very clear idea, not only on who was good on a Cat, but what it cost on average to keep them going. Unfortunately, not all crawler drivers are good ones, and the cost of this, and especially the tracks, kept Bill's eye on the hunt for a viable alternative. Busy though this made him, it didn't stop him teaching engineering at night school and running car maintenance classes for the company staff.

---

* Scottish mud!

In the early 60s the first County 4 was purchased, which proved immediately that it was an able beast on the right timber, despite all the predictions of gloom by the crawler men, who had taken over the mantle of conservatism from the steamies. Initially a special loading sulky was designed for it, which worked well enough on hardwood but not for the Scotch trade, which was largely made up softwood logs of smaller dimensions. The immediate advantage of the Igland winch with two drums and the lightweight grapple crane was recognised.

From small beginnings, and with the co-operation of the Igland family in Norway, and the Jonssons of Cranab in Sweden, the Tapps of County and Mercedes Benz, the Forest Engineering Division of James Jones and Sons started up with Bill Baillie as Chief Engineer. In the years that followed, timber handling machines and logging systems were developed, and these took Bill first round the U.K. and Ireland, then further afield to Canada, the States, Africa, and the Far East.

Bill retired at the end of 1986, but in his later working years spent much of his time, both in the U.K. and abroad, visiting, training, advising, and passing on his vast fund of knowledge and experience of transport and logging systems for the timber industry. Typically, within a month of retiring he was heard to say that he was so busy that he was "looking for an apprentice"!

At the A.P.F. demonstration - Cannock 1988 - I stood spellbound as star operators on two Foden based 'Fiskas' loaders lifted logs from one pile with the precision of a couple of international jugglers, as each log missed the other with perfect timing. The latest from the house of Jones was the enormous Canadian 380 B 'Timberjack' skidder they now distribute. Demonstrator Alan Guild, a big fellow, confirmed she was 22ft long and 10ft 2" wide. One of her uses is with a massive scarifier, preparing the ground for tomorrow's trees.

The single horse, shod with the patent Jones nail, way back in the 1800s, is a far cry from the power of the 148 Cummins horses in this orange beauty! Our timber trade is peppered with inventive innovators, whose proven ideas have been marketed, but James Jones of Larbert tops them all.

Pioneers of Timber

An early Royal Highland Show. note signwritten tree on timberwagon.

Smart of Leith have 15 tons on this Leyland 'Hippo' in 1936. Dick Brown with Fordson and Hesford winch ropes forward to assist. Dick regularly hauled 10 ton loads on 36 mile trips with this Fordson, with his mate seated on the drawbar. These figures, huddled in oilskins, became a legend endemic of their breed.

Contractor James Guild with his TD9 Crawler at Ballindalloch in 1950. Before air conditioning!

One of the 21 Matadors loading a Dyson trailer rafted on Loch Monar.

An ex ministry Foden ropes out the well loaded Dyson.

This hybrid ex naval Foden six wheeler was fitted with the scrapped STG 5 winch and pivoting front axle.

'Never enough road.' An ex WD Albion 6 x 4 slipped off this one.

Three of the early Unimogs converted by James Jones.

A County CD 50
with Boughton
winch and home
made Sulky.

William Ogilvie
stacks a tight load
at Fort William.

Some of the staff and products in the
1970s. These photographs are
courtesy the Bill Baillie collection

IRENE AND DAVE

Few women have enough timber in their blood to stand a 40 mile trip and back, whining along in a 'self willed' 1955 old Latil, the only Latil I have seen with drum brakes in 40 years.

I chatted with Irene and Dave Fry, of Cowfold, as I admired 'Old Smokey' No. CSV 376. Fordsons to Fodens feature in this truly family business, which in the early days consisted of not only the four children but wife and mother-in-law, working in the woods.

Dave concentrated on cutting birch poles for broomheads and Irene knew all about getting a thousand faggots on their then Leyland Mastiff, for besom brooms. Birch poles had to be striped, the term used for removing a strip of bark with a special tool to aid drying out. Irene must have done thousands in her time. In between, she ferried parts and tackle in the firm's service car. This was actually a much bashed and battered old Austin Ascot that Irene was ashamed to be seen in at times. Keeping abreast of all the paper work always was the wife's work in these set-ups, as mine will confirm.

Today, Irene and Dave have sons, Dennis and Simon, taking the strain. They have a Matador, of course, but it was F403 JKR that took my breath away! A brand new custom built Foden double drive. Dave had this kind of lorry built around his big Atlas AK 5002 loader. The Foden, minus trailer, with Atlas, weighs $13^1/_2$ tons. For this the front axle was uprated and chassis reinforced. So what's behind her? A tri axle trailer? Not on your life. A 1967 pole waggon, would you believe? But why, I queried? "Because I carry long timber, and it suits me", said Dave.

The 4 x 4 Fry Sentinel was the other eye opener. About 200 were made in 1954-58, built for the R.A.F. Demobbed in 1970 and now minus her Rolls Royce straight 8 engine, fluid flywheel, twin rear wheels, and aircraft starting generator, at least the 15 ton Darlington winch remains, and power is now provided by a Leyland engine. She carries a Hiab Crane, and churns through mud, far from her native R.A.F. tarmac. In fact, when it's really wet she out-performs the Matador.

Built to pull V Bombers Valiant, Victor and Vulcans, today this Sentinel prefers Veneers, if Dave should be so lucky!

Little family outfits like this are the life blood of our trade and we gladly honour them.

Dave's ex RAF
Sentinel
aircraft towing
tug.

Designed for tarmac,
adapted for mud – this
Sentinel goes where a
Matador won't.

F 403 JKR
Foden 6 x 4
and 1967 pole
trailer with a
load of fine
ash butts.

BEDFORDS - YOU SEE THEM EVERYWHERE

As my grandpa's 'T' Ford became older, Mr Todd, the Ford Salesman, was profuse in his issue of leaflets. Regular copies of the "Ford Times" magazine came straight to me unopened and were treasured for years. Friend Fred Tearle, of Vine Cottage, urged grandpa otherwise. In 1924 Fred had a new 30cwt Chevrolet from the Luton Agents, West End Motors (now an Exhaust Centre) in Dunstable Road. Fred had done 20,000 miles when Ted Willis took the wheel in 1926. By 1931 Ted had clocked about 300,000 miles on this 23 H.P. 4 Cyl. O.H.V. lorry that would do 65 m.p.h. In the fruit season Ted was travelling the 50 mile trip to Cottenham Cambs. three times daily - a longish day. A ton overload was the regular 'norm' and no-one could fault the Chev., or Ted, and his record hours at the wheel. In early 1931 Fred enquired about a new Luton built Chev. and learned a magnificent new lorry called a Bedford 2 tonner was being built at Vauxhall. Therefore, Fred ordered 'Get me the very first you can'. They did, and it is a matter of pride that one of the very first Bedfords came to Eaton Bray. Prior to this, I can just remember being held on grandpa's shoulders in a crowd of people cheering a green lorry as it drove up the steep Blow's Down. Imagine my excitement in 1987 to find a full write-up in the 'Luton News' dated June, 1929. Following the quarter page invite, came photographs and a full report the next week. "Chevrolet Hill Climb Extraordinaire" tells how vehicles thronged Skimpot Lane, Luton, and crowds surged over the railway, and beyond, to the old lime workings still visible halfway up Blow's Down, to the side of the new Tesco building.

A Luton Surveyor said the 440 foot track starts at 1 in $5^1/_2$ and becomes 1 in $3^1/_2$ near the top.

Selected from stock the 26.33 H.P. 6 Cyl. Chevrolet fitted with standard tyres was filled with Pratt's petrol. After loading with 30 and $^3/_4$ cwts of stone, according to the published weigh-bridge ticket, was added weights of Mate and Driver Hickman, who died only recently.

The public, potential customers, the opposition, the nation's motor trade, and press, were all there to 'guesstimate'. 'WILL IT DO IT'? All due to a new low fourth gear, it did, three times, with Hickman stopping and starting on the 1 in $3^1/_2$, to loud cheers. The descents were perfect demonstrations of the new four wheel brakes. The public were invited to feel the 'only warm' radiator cap. Orders rolled in, as did demand for tickets for the film of this event at Luton's Palace Theatre.

Remember this was during the Depression, hence the advertising. I quote -"The Chevrolet 6 Cyls (at the price of 4) is Luton Built, by Luton Men. Trade is bad. Everyone says so, but the Luton Factory is building Chevrolets, working as hard as they can go! Why? Because commercial vehicle owners know their value, and will have no other. Buy Chevrolet, boast it, bank on it." Blow's Downs was put on the motoring map overnight. I understand grandpa was impressed, as was my father, who dreaded blocking the old Ford on Offley Hill to off-load, and carry 18 score boxes of eggs to the top, returning from Royston in all weathers. Fred Tearle, charging past in his Chev, was often the last straw.

When the Chev however was found to have a new-fangled gear lever, grandpa returned to Fords, and to his dismay, this Company had adapted a similar system. Nevertheless, loyal to Fords, he ordered a model 'A' in return for special gear changing lessons, which must have cost the Luton Motor Company a lot of their profit and patience.

However, these words and photographs are intended as a tribute to Bedford. Locally, we do well to remember the 60 years' prosperity we have enjoyed under the umbrella of Vauxhall Motors.

The Blow's Down event was just one of a National Dealer promotion called "Coats off" for Chevrolet Month.

Twenty-two hill climbs were staged from Porlock to 3,000 feet up Skiddaw. The list included Rest-and-be-Thankful, Mow Cop, Box Hill, Devils Dyke etc. Attendances ranged from 500 at Blow's to 12,000 at a Chatham military test track. Biggest sales were 33, a whole train load to Aberdeen.

One enterprising dealer, who had no hills in his area, advertised a 'Talking Chevrolet' at the County Show. He mounted a loudspeaker under the bonnet, and a salesman, with a microphone in a sheet under the vehicle. A spellbound crowd listened to the spiel about this British built truck that claimed a new Carter carb., Delco ignition, handsome dashboard. "Try my sprung seats", the Chev requested. "My cost is £230, with dropsides, and tax only £20", it continued. Then the dealer invited questions from the crowd, which he repeated loudly to the lorry. "Yes I enjoy being overloaded" a farmer was told.

All a bit corny 60 years on, but revolutionary then.

Dealers vied with each other for promotional prizes, and I note even the Managing Director of heavy lorry builders, Commer Cars, congratulated Chevs on the Blow's Down climb.

Dealers were urged to have the events filmed and shown at the local cinema. People like to see themselves, and predicted sales were clinched. Harry Brown had ordered a six-wheeler and a Buick car at Blow's Down, and offered to show the film free at "The Oriel" cinema he owned in Leighton Buzzard. The projector was via a belt driven generator.

Charlie Nash of Leighton Buzzard remembers when the film slowed down, the operator would rush black treacle on the slipping belt! Happy Days!! Harry Pool, also of Leighton Buzzard, went into haulage and found a 3 ton Bedford was comfy with 5. Requiring a 'trade-in' price, the worn out lorry was first loaded with a scrap car. Shaw & Kilburn were cajoled into putting another £5 into the deal, but refused to off-load the heap of rust. Three years later Harry repeated the stunt, on a fresh salesman. When the former one appeared, he exploded with "don't let him put that wreck in the deal, it's already ours. Take it to the tip"! Likewise, grandpa would make a final offer, drive off, leaving his drover's stick behind, then return for it in a few minutes and re-open negotiations on the deal.

The new Bedford was the sensation of the 1931 Motor Show.

Brothers Don and Gordon Wood, Haulage Contractors of Twyford, Bucks, ordered one on the stand, the first of many.

The story of the 'Cream Express' explains why.

A daunting task for the brothers was to run two loads of cream a day from Buckingham to Chard, Somerset, up until the war. Using the same lorry DPP 585, doing almost 600 miles a day, and night, 10 times a week, with two drivers, come rain, fog, or snow, the Bedford never let them down. Their other three tonner was on local milk collection and is similar to our own Bill Wright's famous Bedford that collected farm milk and was fitted with seats for Luton Football Patrons' Saturday afternoons.

The first record of a Jellis in haulage is when Reg's great grandfather was commissioned to remove the bodies of two gamekeepers murdered in Aldbury woods in 1891. Reg's parents were butchers of Pitstone, Bucks. Their first Bedford, a cattle truck in 1959, led into General Haulage. A switch from cement transport to livestock, via a demountable body, ended with an outbreak of foot and mouth disease.

Born and bred on Bedford, covering 340,000 miles himself on a favourite 'T.K.' and with a beautifully restored W.S. type, this man is pro Bedford. Yet today, a splendid Atkinson heads his immaculate fleet. Like so many of his contemporaries, he had deserted the Bedford fold, with reluctance. Another man who helped build the foundations of Bedford, was Major H.P. Mitchell of Trudoxhill, Frome. Three 2 ton flats carried 5 ton loads of pit props daily, for eleven years. Even the newish 10 year old had 300,000 miles behind her. They were towed in and out of tortuous woods best suited to a 'Q.L.'. Understandably drivers were adept at road spring fittings. A hard road questioner wondered why they traversed a gully with one foot on the throttle and one on the running board, and was smartly told - "So we can jump of course".

Hundreds of the 50,000 'Q.L.' 4 x 4 came into timber.

One man bought half an acre of them, as he put it.

Two were fitted with elaborate jibs and anchors, then as their engines succumbed, the front end was cut off behind the cab and replaced by a fresh front end from the field, retaining only the number plate and seat cushion. The act of grafting became such an art, it was done in less time than some of you take to change a tractor power fork for a bucket.

Fred Tearle's 1921 Chevrolet, snapped with Cambridge customers.

The Luton Motor Company, March 1931. New commercial vehicles await delivery on the forecourt, Beech Hill, Luton. Courtesy The Luton News.

Chipping Norton Carnival. Tom Stanley claimed "I had most models of Bedfords as they came along, not new of course but after a few years".

INVITATION TO ALL

Commercial Vehicle Owners and Drivers

on

WEDNESDAY NEXT, JUNE 26th

AT 3 P.M.

A standard 30 cwt. Chevrolet will be driven, fully loaded, up steep grassy side of Blow's Down (opposite Houghton Regis Turning, half way to Dunstable). We invite you to witness this proof of the amazing capabilities of the world's best 30 cwt. lorry, the £230 lorry with 6 cylinders, four speed gear box, four wheel brakes, and 20 other improvements.

A film will be taken for exhibition at the Palace Theatre, Luton, from Monday, July 1st, to Saturday, July 6th. All people interested please fill in coupon below entitling you to free pass to Palace Theatre during the above week.

This lorry mounted hoarding toured the district in June 1929. Courtesy of the Luton News.

The 1 in 3¹/₂ certified gradient attempt on Blow's Down begins. Courtesy of the Luton News.

Unipower Ltd. convert an early Bedford to double drive. Courtesy Mr. T. Powell.

Unipower Ltd., Bedford and Ford 6 wheeled demonstrators. Courtesy Mr. T. Powell.

James Jones' Carrimore artic loaded with peeled larch bark in 1936.

'The Cream Express' overturns in Rode, Somerset. Gordon and Don Wood patched her up and actually drove her home. I spent many happy hours reminiscing with the late Don Wood, who retired to Eaton Bray.

*Chloe and
Charles Jellis
sold hot
chitterlings from
this van for 7d a
pound in Eaton
Bray.*

*George Croasdale
in Rydel Park,
Haverthwaite.*

*200 86 feet long larch were
ordered for Barrow
shipyard scaffolding.
George Croasdale's
Bedford was converted to a
long artic with high back
bolster to clear the walls on
cornering. All done on
Cumbrian hills with more
nerve than h.p. (only 27).*

Still at work in 1951, the Bedford 5-tonner receives about 10 tons as grandfather Croasdale looks on.

One of Major Mitchell's 2-tonners that took 5 tons daily for eleven years.

Stemp's Perkins engined Bedford. Note the Perkins emblem that reflects "A square deal all round".

The Tyrell Racing Organisation Ltd. was conceived and born in the Tyrell's timber yard at Ocham, Surrey. Here Ken stands beside a fine oak butt, backgrounded by Hereford Cathedral.

One of 2 tractor units built to transport Bedfords own 40 ton dies on a solid tyred Eagle low loader between Luton and Dunstable. Douglas Equipment H.D. rear axles with 900 x 20 tyres were driven through two speed transfer boxes. Only Vauxhall could afford to use petrol engines on heavy haulage in 1965. Photograph courtesy of Peter Davies (The man whose painting on the cover of SORTH gave the book such impact).

OUR COCKNEY COUSINS

The first character in the 'Yull' photograph album goes back five generations, and is armed with a mattock. This symbolises a remarkable family firm of urban foresters and tree-surgeons in London, where the tree game is the same, but all the rules are different.

Maximum power and ability to operate in confined areas is a daily demand of both machines, and the six man team of the brothers Malcolm and Peter Yull, with sons Matthew, Steven and Paul and a lad, Philip. Malcolm explained his obsession for the Bedford Q.L. "They just go on, and on, and on," he repeated.

Arthur Yull, father, had bought 12 Q.L.s at a sale. One is in a Cornish museum. Nine were used and abused, then cannibalised for spares, then all were later sold and used in a war film once, being blown up. Two are still at work!

Malcolm has driven 513 VMC for 35 years, and treats her like a family pet. She took over from the Matador as work areas diminished in size, and 5 engines later she is now ready for her sixth. One engine died pulling a big tree over a tight spot in the Kings Road, Chelsea. Just getting a tree up to vertical when half the crankshaft drops on the floor and the fan pulley flies through the radiator is not the time to hear "Keep pulling, she's all yours"!

Her sister, the other Q.L., stumped me.

Had it been Dunstable Downs, haunt of AWD testing, I would have suspected a David Brown prototype. A TK cab part covered a tight-fitting engine from a 'D' reg 16 ton Bedford artic. This required disposing of the handbrake disc and front drive shaft, welding the two couplings back to back, and chopping two feet out of the rear shaft. The result is a tractor with Land Rover like wheelbase. The 'get away' of a sports car, up to 50 m.p.h., God and half shafts willing, and a Latil-like turning circle, that tows their big Vermeer stump grinder into the most awkward sites.

The album is packed with press cuttings, and prints of trees lowered limb by limb within the constrictions of bricks and mortar. Three Ford Transits with Yull designed features nip around London's traffic like taxis.

Their Woodchipper I thought a luxury is a must, running 75 decibels in unison with three of four chainsaws reverberating round concrete confines, leaves us little to envy our cockney cousins.

Years ago a trade delegation at the Russian Embassy was expecting the Yulls for tree work. When two, still militarised Q.L.s and an ex-Army Austin swung in there, they turned out the full armed guard. Not knowing the Russian for 'Ruddington', Malcolm brandished their chainsaws to show World War Three was not really on the cards!

During World War Two this family carried a record cubeage of round timber from Norfolk to London on several Crossley artics that did 4 m.p.g. To save a drop of petrol, each unit always towed another back light to Norfolk, despite the 75 foot train length.

Grandfather was a winter woodcutter, who cycled with his scythe each summer up to Norfolk to cut laid corn.

Later, this man did a London wood round, riding pillion on his son's motor bike, seated back to back, holding the handles of a Coster's barrowfull of logs. I looked again at the two Q.L.s. It seems initiative runs in this family and appears in every generation.

In 1958, Yulls undertook to transplant several mature plane trees in the Mall. Since they weighed 6 tons plus, they were lifted with their Matador and a stabiliser (a block of wood under the anchor). The cab was filled with chains and scrap iron and four men stood on the bumper each quarter mile precarious trip, as the police escort looked the other way.

Arthur Yull (never seen without his cap or a Woodbine), centre, with the root-laden Chev. in 1930. The practise was to grub a tree with the Fordson, dig in and back the Chev. under the root so that it fell on the lorry when cut.

The famous QL Malcolm has driven for 35 years.

THE RUDDINGTON REGULAR

Never bet the Potter Brothers they don't know every nut on an ex W.D. Bedford!! It could lose you money, I'm told.

I met John and Henry Potter among a sea of Bedfords at the former Railway Station, Singleton, Sussex. These men have specialised in Land Rover and Bedford re-builds here for years - from Gritters and Snow Ploughs to tropical Cabs. Their self-built Bedford Fork Lift Truck, operated from within a TK cab, leaves me in no doubt of the ingenuity of timber men. Harry Potter started hauling in North Bersted, near Bognor, in 1939. His first Bedford was a flat 3 tonner which he later converted to an artic pole trailer. With the demise of this a 1937 3 tonner took over the pole trailer and 8 ton loads. The first Q.L. gave 30,000 miles of trouble free hauling. Doing 2 loads a day, 256 miles from London docks to Cocking with 10 to 12 tons of Obeche up, says something for Q.L.s and John Potter at the wheel. Soon they had 2 Q.L. artics on the road, often 7 days a week. As each Q.L. wore out it was replaced with a fresh one from the vast Potter stocks. Harry Potter attended the first, and every Ruddington sale. He bought Bedfords in Germany 80 at a time, including the first ex Army R.L., price £650, with 630 miles on the clock, and ran it 6 years. By 1965 Harry's securing of his own spares had become a stock pile for others. Timber haulage ceased and the old goods yard looked like an annexe of Vauxhall Motors.

Now I digress a little. It's no secret now, or then, that the German ³/₄ track gun tractor was second to none, as we found to our cost in the western desert. When several were captured in Libya, the Ministry of Supply had them brought to Vauxhall Motors, stripped down, and given full military trials. Then came the War Office directive to design and develop a British equivalent, designated the 'B.T.' (Bedford Tractor). Six prototypes were built in just over a year, but production was halted when V.E. day came. I talked with Alan Green, who performance tested the 'Praga' vehicle the 'B.T.' was based on. In the absence of time to develop a new engine, 2 standard 28 h.p. engines were geared together, mounted side by side, in front of a single clutch. Vauxhall already had its own Churchill Tank testing course, next door in Luton Hoo Park. A sand pit provided excellent field trial conditions. The 'B.T.' would climb a one in two gradient, wade through up to six feet of water and average 25 m.p.h. on the road, fully loaded, towing a gun. The track steering brakes gave Alan a few hairy moments in traffic. He also remembers the Bedford 96 mile run across the Chilterns. The apprentice tester was always given the heavy ended Q.L.R. wireless truck, keeping up with the others sorted the men from the boys. Returning to the Potters, when three 'B.T.s' turned up at Ruddington, Harry snapped them up. True, one had no tracks but the runner was taxed and soon hard at work at Chiddingfold, Surrey. This operation ended suddenly, for two reasons. One was the Potters' idea of a fair load for the 'B.T.', whose clutch burnt out as a Vauxhall V.I.P. arrived, stating the three vehicles were still on the War Office secret list and had been released for sale in error. In no time Harry was left with only his official receipt of ownership, which he used to endeavour to get a new car from the embarrassed company, but their derisory compensation fell far short of this. At least it was another Potter record. Who else had hauled timber with a State Secret?

One of these QLs was fitted with a 'Big Bedford' diesel engine, to which the halfshafts objected.

Rolling them on.

Loaded and away.

Derek Goatman of
Vauxhall Motors with the
'Trap Clap', as the Potters
nicknamed this B.T.
equipped with a 5 ton winch
and Cletrac-type steering.

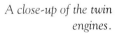

A close-up of the twin
engines.

THE BORN AGAIN GRIFFIN

The emblem of the mythological Griffin with its Eagle's Head, Wings and Claws on a Lion's body emblazoned on the radiator of Bedford Lorries, goes back to the 13th century in Luton.

Once upon a time Bedfords were number one in Britain, and the Griffin reigned supreme. I'm not sure when it started to ail, but by 1987 the Griffin was sick unto death. Many top motor medics made pronouncements, but none came up with a cure. A great cloud was hanging over the people of Luton and Dunstable when Doctor David Brown came down from the north. A thorough examination was made of the anaemic creature, now on a life support machine.

The case history notes bulged with attacks of 'Detroit Thirst' and Nightmare Cabs for a mechanic seeking an elusive engine in the 1970s. Even the parents gave up on it, concentrating on the healthy members of the family. In fact, the starved (of investment) Griffin was up for adoption, but no-one wanted to know.

Something at the forlorn Boscombe Road Factory touched the Doctor, who emerged from 'intensive care', prescribing a series of heavy (cash) injections, and a course of a drug called New-Markets. "They're not over the counter, we must make them ourselves", he declared.

First the haemorrhage of hope among the work-force was stemmed, and the diet of obsolete design changed. New laurels were sought, since 'resting on old ones' was another cause of the trouble. As the patient perked up, it was re-named 'All Wheel Drive'. The Griffin excelled at being a 4 x 4. Why not a 6 x 6. Or even 8 x 8? The possibilities were tremendous.

Then there came a great race, for which the Griffin trained round the clock. Sadly the judges favoured a part outsider and there was much licking of sores, followed by the sharpening of claws. At least the Griffin made his rivals sweat, and there will always be another day.

Well there is nothing mythological about David Brown. When he bought Bedford Trucks, a rugged old northern timberman said - "If anyone can sort 'em out, Matt's boy will".

John Brown & Sons steam engines were known across the north. Sons William and Denis drove steam tractors from Darlington to Sussex, carrying out major repairs on tram lines in central London. Brother Matthew, who stayed north, had a brilliant logging I.Q.

He needed to have, his tackle left much to be desired. He was plagued with above his share of adverse conditions, the natural habitat of timbermen.

The boy David found he could skid out 40 cube on an old Fordson, ingeniously lifting the butt ends, long before jibs and logging arches. Much of this man's design had been from sheer necessity. The articulated tractor, as we know it in the U.K., was his brainchild. When it comes to Multidrive, David Brown designed and built 8 wheel drive tractors for Muir-Hill to export over 20 years ago. His 8 x 8, 25 ton with rear wheel steer, eliminating tyre scrub, is a fantastic proven concept of cross country and the highway transport. Ironically, the law has been adjusted for it, as it was for Matt's first Lanchester artic in 1929.

There is a great similarity between David Brown and the late Viscount Montgomery. Both men faced rallying disheartened people, with unorthodox plans of attack, liaised with their subordinates, and each lost their first big battle. As for 'Monty', he listed his successes, then announced "We will reinforce success with success, and victory will be ours", and it was!! At Boscombe Road they have re-grouped with a line of civilian down to earth trucks that will knock the opposition cold. That old Logger was right, Matt's boy is sorting 'em out!

Everybody remembers Henry Ford.

The name of William Durant, founder of General Motors, is far less known. After 12 years, he was pushed off the Board he had created. He then lost 40 million dollars trying to build his own cars in the depression, and died almost broke in 1947.

In Flint, Michigan, U.S.A. in 1988, a monument was unveiled to William Durant. In the tribute it was said - "We are still eating from the bountiful table he gave us, although we have forgotten his name".

A splendid action photograph of the AWD 8 x 8 25-tonner multidrive on test at Millbrook, Beds.

THE PROFESSIONALS

Undoubtedly, I have met and made scores of friends in and through the Association of Professional Foresters.

It started with their 1985 Conference where, as a guest speaker on the top table, two dear ladies, Pam Miller and Shirley Richmond, took turns in mopping my fevered brow!

Thanks to free access at all A.P.F. events, thousands have come to know about 'CORDA', the heart charity to which I have dedicated the rest of my days. I am indeed indebted to Pam and Mike Miller for their subtle, yet forceful promotions, of my books. The same must be said of Secretary, Tony Philips. A man who, when the word 'green' was just a colour, pioneered closing the chasm of the Timberman's image of a chainsaw wielding depredator of the countryside to that of one who plants, tends, and harvests a diminishing resource. His 80-acre Woodland Park and Lake at Brokerswood, Westbury, Wilts, is a living example of the blending of forestry management, wildlife, leisure, and outdoor enjoyment, midst good timber husbandry. His O.B.E. for service to forestry was richly deserved. The popular myth of forest rape and timber barons is no longer a reality to the 20,000 visitors a year there.

A character, old Hoppy Gates, came across a conservationist in the 1950s. It was a lady sitting under a tree in a deck chair. The local Bobby had told the tree fellers only 'verbal force' was in order. This proved strong, but pointless. Hoppy quietly drew his Latil into the prevailing wind, set a fast tick over and pumped his oil can into the air intake. The lady disappeared midst clouds of smoke and Hoppy sat in the deck chair as the tree was felled. The Constable was displeased, but Hoppy insisted - "I was only freeing a sticking valve". As for the "Greenhouse effect", this was first observed by a Tree Surgeon, who perfectly roped and lowered every limb of a huge tree that overhung a greenhouse, then dropped his lopping saw through it, as he was coming down, to the applause of the onlookers!

But I digress, once more.

I attended the bi-annual Forest Machinery Demonstration (the largest in Europe) at Cannock Chase, in 1988. A magnificent three day event organised solely by Members themselves, who give up chunks of their holidays, and lives, to promote our industry.

A team of 10 member co-ordinators manned the site on Honda runabouts, under the direction of Roger Fitter, a big man in so many ways. Stories abound of rebuilding the loading ramp in car headlights; the Becraig's site where four inches of rain had to be channelled off via a trench dug through the refreshments tent; the Health and Safety Officer, who drove his car through protective tapes into a roped-off bog; the big low-loader that took a short cut over Lord Lonsdale's lawn. Security was so tight, one member's wife was apprehended by a patrol for not carrying her pass when she popped from her caravan to the loo, during the night!

I qualified for a Press Release Officer, Patricia Orr, who introduced endless V.I.P.s to my book, and 'CORDA' display.

Our President's wife, Lady Clinton, had me wondering if I should curtsy or bow. At least I didn't introduce her to Lord Clinton, as someone did. Everyone who is anyone in timber attends this vast modern machinery marathon. I braced myself to meet forest owner Terry Wogan, but alas he must have been working on his Matador that week!

Sales of my book aided the A.P.F. Provident Fund, as did the raffle tickets. Mike Miller helped pressurise the punters into £3,778 worth.

I have such happy memories of sharing the rich fellowship of the lumber 'Jills and Jacks' of today.

MERRIST WOOD EXTRAVAGANZA

My old friend John Harraway invited me to be a guest of the Arboricultural Association's Extravaganza held at Merrist Wood, near Guildford in July, 1989. A group of people, dedicated to raise and maintain highest standards of tree work across the land, were celebrating 25 years of caring for trees. Trade Stands, ancient and modern, and timber equipment were the background of an open day. The public arrived by cars, and sadly stayed in them, in this, the wettest Saturday afternoon of the summer.

Oblivious of the rain, teams of steaming young bodies hand winched tractors 30 yards in relays, hand crosscut trees, climbed spars and covered an assault course, throwing loaded barrows of logs over a fence, in a kind of forestry royal tournament. Worst of all, these teams were verbally lashed and abused 'Tannoy Wise' by a vivacious young lady named 'Penny', known to some of us. Seven old Matadors turned up in all their dirt and went about their business, minus any rally 'tart-up'.

Sussex Timberman, Bernard Patience, attended with his gorgeous Unipower 'Hannibal', and gave me a turn at the wheel. What a joyous day this was!

BUT FORTY YEARS AGO...

There were no modern tree surgery aids for me in the 1950s. The simple procedure to fell or lop a roadside tree was a red flag stuck in an old 5 gallon drum, down traffic of the operation. I would saw off a few branches to keep vehicles at bay. Next, before lopping saws, one Bow sawed perhaps for 20 minutes, as my trusty assistant Jim, or Helen, controlled single line traffic with the flag. At the first creak I'd shout "hold 'em", then saw like 'the clappers', always dreading the idiot who would stop underneath to ask "are they felling it". Once I had a tree across the road, and my reluctant new 'Danarm Saw' died on me. A policeman caught in the traffic build up, advised signs, and notice to close the road in future.

One day I under-priced a large Elm. All the brushwood was stacked high around my Douglas jib, and down over the cab. It looked like a Forestry Commission entry in a carnival. My big trailer's twin tyres were rubbing under the weight of the cordwood, and still top wood remained in the road. A policeman, collecting the signs in a 'Black Maria', admired the logs. Ever the opportunist, the 'B.M.' was loaded with logs. It was my gesture for all the police help, I maintained! Next time I asked for signs, the point was made: "strictly no logs please, you broke a spring last time". A memorable job was felling a tree on a canal towpath without vehicle access, at Croxley Green, Herts. John Dickinson's Paper Mills were opposite, and at first no burning-up insurance cover was available. Then a small fire was agreed, providing 'J.D.s' fire-pump was running on stand by. I had just lit up when a 'hose happy' fireman knocked me down with a jet of water, drenching the area. Then 'Jesus' appeared, a character so called because of his long flowing beard. This man had a firewood yard along the two-path, 60 yards away, and wanted to buy wood. This was offered free if he would take the brushwood also. The plan was to tush the logs along with his mangey old mare. This worked, until impatiently I cut the logs bigger each time. Helen had just said "You'll kill that horse" as it strained in the collar, when a trace chain broke and plunged it straight into the canal. It took all three of us, pulling on the rein of the frightened animal, as it swam, paddled, and walked, to a shallow spot down stream.

Jesus, and his horse, never returned. The wood was stacked, thrown into the canal by children overnight, as we found to our relief next day.

Cannock Chase, 1988. The James Jones 380 B 'Timberjack' – 10 feet wide, 22 feet long – towers above the APF members that virtually co=ordinate their own show. These people, seen and unseen, have given me great pleasure in my retirement. Photograph courtesy of Andy Hutchings.

The one time popular 'Cleland' conversion, made by Sennocke Engineering, Sevenoaks, Kent. Incorporating a Cooke two speed winch and radiator grille that housed counter weights and trailer vacuum tank. John Heath tests his Fordson here after restoration.

Bob Price of Tilsworth was ploughing with his Marshall Crawler. After an explosion, Bob was left looking down on the piston. It seems a counter weight had come off the crankshaft. Photograph courtesy of Stuart Abraham.

Ted Petts of St. Albans was the first man I remember stump grinding in the Home Counties. Friend Steve Russell sent this action photograph. The tow truck is a shortened crew cab International 4 x 4, probably USAF built to UK spec. Now re-engined with a Perkins 643, a smart motor indeed.

This Latil agricultural tractor won a ploughing contest in Ireland circa 1927. In fact it was so wet it became the only machine to move from the starting line. Photograph courtesy of Bernard Berrows.

Reg. U7645. The first self loading artic. Stuart (Broadleaf) Brown's great grandfather drove this steamer for Bartletts from High Wycombe to Hampshire regularly, where he met his wife. 'Broadleaf' roots are long established in timber!

M.A.N., MATADOR AND MUSIC

Peter Noyce rang from Wiltshire, with kind words about my books, purchased it seems from Edlesborough Post Office.

When I cleared the trees for Heathermead Homes, I little dreamed that in several years' time Rose-Marie and Peter Allen would open up whole new vistas of organ music for my delight, in their Meadside abode.

The lynchpin of this story is Peter Noyce's son, young Robert, who is also hooked on organs of every kind, and met the Allens at St. Albans Organ Museum.

The centenary of the Noyce family timber business was in 1980. Four brothers ran the sawmill their grandfather founded at West Tytherley, Wilts. Edward Noyce was into Spar or Rick Peg making. One, Tom Broomfield, cut them under a sheet in the woods, until he died, aged 90.

In World War One, Edward Noyce held a big contract to supply bavins (faggots) for the Army Field Kitchens on Salisbury Plain. A wide range of timbers were milled by the brothers, hauled on various vehicles, but in their heyday an AEC Mercury and four Mandators headed the fleet. Today, cousins, and partners, Michael and Peter, with their Loader Driver of many years, Martin Wieland, are solely in timber haulage, with two 'M.A.N.' tractor units.

As for Robert Noyce, electronics and organs are his scene, the latter being a gift that deserves exploitation. When this lad's left leg aches, it's from gliding across a 32-note pedalboard and not a Matador clutch pedal. Not for Robert the muck and mud of timber. His pride and joy is a three manual Theatre-voiced Electronic Organ, built into a solid oak console of an ex Church organ.

Robert played some part in the design and construction of this magnificent instrument, that was re-born in the workshop of top electronic organ builder, Bill Walker.

In 1988, Robert was sponsored by the St. Albans Organ Museum to attend a course for organists who showed future potential. The exercise required a spell on the ex Trocadero, Elephant and Castle, Europe's largest WurliTzer. This to some of you is tantamount to a van driver being publicly confronted with a 16 speed gearbox, and all such H.G.V. driving entails. Imagine then an audience anticipating the blunders of missed or crashed gears and you will know how well Robert did to coax a few decent sounds from this king of instruments, the organ, which creates the biggest sound any one musician can make. As the big names step down from the console, some prematurely, like Ernest Broadbent, of Blackpool fame, it's refreshing to know a nucleus of young people thrive in the nursery of theatre organ music. Peter and Jenny Noyce must listen with considerable pride to Robert. This young man might just bring up the console to Nelson Elm's signature tune 'Trees', but that is as near to timber as we are likely to see him!

Bowler-hatted Edward Noyce with a 5 horse team. A hundred years ago it was horses that got ear protection. Liquid refreshment was supplied, I note.

The location and men in this marvellous picture are not known. The load is rather more than the intended 4 tons by Leyland. This was the late 1920s in the day of the bulb horn, and prior to tyre tread regulations, it appears.

Another Leyland Noyce's favoured. The dual purpose hook on pole trailer and removable front bolster.

This Surrey Dodge also served on pulpwood cart and crawler transport when the bolster would be turned between the tracks.

The Albion's petrol engine was replaced with a 5LW diesel. New in 1943, the ERF was the wagon Peter learned to drive in.

This Matador gave sterling service as an artic.

In the mill, a skilled eye can 'middle a tree' first time when hooking up.

One of the four well loaded Mandators. A Matador lurks up the road.

The two M.A.N. team today. Cousins and partners Peter and Michael Noyce. How refreshing to see sign written vehicle names today – 'Jumbo' and 'Herman' – even a 747 jet in flight.

Dare you lift a case of £4,000 plus delicate electronics with your Matador?

Peter Noyce and organ builder Bill Walker fix protective packing.

An impatient young Robert Noyce sits at the console.

WurliTzer
- THE NAME THAT MEANS
MUSIC TO MILLIONS!!

Have you ever considered a world void of all music? Your kind of music - be it Boogie, Bach, Beatles, Beethoven, massed choirs and bands, the music of Mancini, Madonna, or Manilow, whatever your choice. Music features from our first nursery rhymes and carols to something more sombre as the curtains draw across the catafalque. A sailor named 'Foort R' lifted the spirits of his shipmates in the battle of Jutland with music. Ralph Reader utilised music in the Scout Movement. Dame Vera Lynn united thousands of loved ones with it. Foden's bus and band went 2,000 miles across war torn Europe with it. Music expresses our every emotion.

In the 1930s, a musically orientated Christian assembly called The Brotherhood, met every Sunday afternoon in Eaton Bray day school. Adults sat on desks, and thrilled to a fine orchestra of violins. Three girls and about seven lads were conducted by Bernard Newman, Schoolmaster (Violinist), 'Getliffe' had arranged a bulk purchase, and Miss Audrey Gray of "Westleigh" (now Doctor Jones' home), became a tutor of high repute. Our front room was a forest of music stands when they practised here, and as the house rang to the sounds of 'Marche Militaire', I vowed one day to join my brother, Eric, with the others. In due course a violin was bought. I never progressed beyond my first tune, 'The Blue Bells of Scotland'. Relentless practice was of no avail. Towards the end Miss Gray left the room (to weep, I imagine) whilst I did my stuff. One day she explained, 'I've spoken to your mother, and you are to rest the violin for a while'. To this day I have heard no more from her! As with my voice, I had a belly full of music but it had a bad road out.

By now the lush sounds of Reginald Foort at the theatre organ flowed from the B.B.C. (and Radio Luxembourg, sponsored by Maclean's toothpaste).

Having become a fan, my mother sent off a 'Radio Times' coupon for a signed photograph. I have it still. These interests were renewed on holiday at Cliftonville in the 1950s, listening to Tony Savage (on a Compton Electrone) for hours. Our eldest daughter, Margaret, was also keen. We heard of, and attended, the opening of the WurliTzer in Buckingham Town Hall in 1963. From then on we were hooked. We joined the Theatre Organ Club and Cinema Organ Society, two excellent organisations that promote concerts wherever organs still play. At some venues, private tape recording was permitted. I remember turning up in the gallery of Watford Town Hall with my £20 domestic Phillips machine, among all the Ferographs and other £200 units. As the Organist touched the keys to play, I pressed the 'play back' instead of record button, and blasted the hall with Dixon I had recorded from the radio. Margaret shot down under the seat. I switched off, and joined her. In the 'Gents' later a patron said "Good Concert" - I agreed. "That twit in the gallery wants shooting" he continued. Again I agreed.

By now Margaret had turned from the piano to the organ at Chapel. I shall ever be indebted to one John Foskett, who allowed Margaret access to the console of, and later arranged lessons on, the Buckingham WurliTzer, where we were attending concerts regularly. A career in the electronic market was being considered. The local Hammond Organ dealer was impressed with Margaret's playing, and the plan was to demonstrate, and endeavour to sell organs from home. When Hammond U.K. said no, I was furious, I reversed the old adage and declared 'If I can't join them - I'll beat them'. We will get our own agency, a statement easier made than executed. Since there was no WurliTzer dealer for fifty miles, this company was the obvious choice. The gist of the reply to my letter was that they were in fact seeking a dealer here, but with a music store, and not the local tree-feller. Undeterred, I visited Alfred Smith, Managing Director of WurliTzer U.K. in Wilmslow, Cheshire, a man who knew the organ business inside out. Enthusiasm, and a twelve-year-old daughter, who could play the odd tune were no qualification, but that was all I had. If anything 'swung it' it was WurliTzer's keenness to have Luton-based George Blackmore's name linked with their electronic, as it was with their pipe organs. A six month trial agency was agreed, stocking only the smallest model. WurliTzer financed the opening show in the National Schools in 1965. George Blackmore came over to try out the limited little organ. "The musical output won't penetrate beyond the second row" he claimed, and loaned his own speaker cabinet, wired in by his engineer Dave Johnson, who was a great tower of strength, as we learned the trade the hard way. One promotional idea was to put Margaret on with G.B. The customer needs to hear the professional, but then protests "but I'll never play like that", or "does he come with the organ"? A few wrong notes from a child beginner never came amiss. The hall was packed. Back stage, midst Margaret's fingernails, hopelessly out of my depth, pumping more adrenalin than it ever took to fell any tree, it was minutes to curtain up. I was in a proper tizzy! At this moment George asked for a chair for his wife. Only 'me' could give her the last one in the house, a broken one, with imaginable results. Another mistake was to get a furnisher to loan a suite to create a drawing room scene on stage. In spite of an impeccable performance from both organists, the only thing sold that night was our name, and an armchair, which had the delighted furnisher asking about the next show. Alfred Smith was impressed, in spite of our fruitless start. "Book Luton Town Hall, and I'll put in G.B. and three back up organs on loan" he suggested. "Make one of them the big theatre job that only tours your star dealers, and you're on", I argued. First I plastered Luton with misprinted posters that implied that George Blackmore, and not the organ, was 'new to Bedfordshire from the States'. So much for the chapter on 'handling the professional organist' in my Dealer's manual. The big organ was diverted from a tour of Ireland. Two hours before the show, as the driver brought it down on the auto tail lift, he questioned 'did we intend to play it, since it was dropped at the docks'? The much travelled console showed signs of the drop, and inside was a mass of unsoldered joints. Of course no 'pro' will touch any instrument not in mint condition, and George felt it was neither fair to himself or WurliTzer to play it. Had all my sweat been in vain? I virtually begged him to try. Dave still soldering inside shouted: "Providing George doesn't open the show with 'The Sabre Dance', he may get through one number". Just a few notes into 'Under the Double Eagle', both organ and organist were in real trouble. George's fingers darted from one set of stops to another as families of voices died, then spasmodically revived. Yet thanks to his dexterity, few knew just how much trouble that organ was in. 'B and G Transport' were to collect the big organ at 9 a.m. next day. At 11 a.m. a Town Hall official asked me to either pay further hall hire, or move onto the pavement. A policeman arrived at 2 p.m. Someone had reported a suspicious man scanning the traffic for an apparent 'get-away' van. Come 5.30 p.m., fed up, famished, and wondering about lamps for my £1,600 charge, the van arrived. My friendly greeting was met with "Look, mate, I've been diverted from Norwich for you. I've got a busted arm, and no auto tail lift! Where's your folk anyway"? Providentially, two passing 'paddies' almost hurtled the 'pain' and me on board.

I registered our company 'Home Electronic Organs'. It was stipulated that it must not be associated with tree work, but inevitably folk would say "I thought you were a tree man", or "Aren't you in organs"?

The big store rat race was not for me. Our Farm Journal adverts ran 'We bring you the roar of the chainsaw by day, and the WurliTzer by night". This was virgin sales territory, and we milked it dry. Dave Johnson came up with a simple group lesson course, the only one in fifty miles. Our WurliTzer Owner's Club was the first in the U.K. A soft, but steady means of selling. We sold most organs between ten and midnight!

I first drooled to the sounds of Len Rawle when he did the 'warm up' for a concert at the A.B.C. Richmond. Much of our success came from his artistry. He played many shows for us, including our, and his, first Yamaha Show. An earthy approach to farmers, plus an ability to deliver organs in 'wellies' across muddy farm yards, gave us an edge on the competition. Not too many had this facility idea, or a Land Rover.

The 'Two Hats' of my occupations saw me complete tree work, wash, brush up, and emerge from the toilets, in various towns, as Mr WurliTzer, to canvass music shops. I frequently felled until 3 p.m., then drove 150 miles to Wilmslow for organs. I would eat and sleep in nearby Ringway airport, and be on the WurliTzer doorstep for 8 a.m. To keep Bedfordshire's sole agency for this prestigious organ, our sales target was raised each year, and we topped it.

In the trade, rumour had it I was a wealthy contractor who sold organs for a hobby! Only the last bit was true.

The mention of "Hammond" was like a red rag to a bull. References to brand 'H' were hushed and wisely kept from my ears at 'The Music Room', my home studio. In 1968 I was invited to a four day WurliTzer seminar in Germany.

Previously I had never flown, stayed in a hotel, or met my fellow dealers, most of whom were at a loss to grasp my unorthodox approach to organ sales. After a session in the hard American sell, we had to cope with our speaker, who acted the awkward client. I got lowest marks of all for talking him down to an organ he could afford, instead of up, to one he couldn't. One afternoon I enjoyed an outing to a brewery only because I left the guided tour to watch a 'Unimog' pulling trees opposite.

WurliTzer's biggest dealers in Europe, J. Van Urk of Rotterdam, showed a cine film of their many operations. When they cut from their super music stores to a D.A.F. articulated mobile showroom that toured villages, markets, and shows, I instantly knew where my future lay. The helpful Van Urk staff confirmed this unique rural promotion. I milked them on every aspect. My jet-setting ended first with doing a 'ton-up' with an organist in his Porsche. Next, a mix-up led to eight of us having no driver for our airport-bound mini bus. An Irish dealer took the wheel, midst a chorus of juggernaut air horns blasting as he tried different lanes! His qualification to volunteer it seems was only that "He didn't trust any of us".

The nearest I could afford to the Van Urk DAF was a 14 foot caravan that I converted to our Mobile Studio. Len Rawle gave us a tremendous launch at a Steam Rally. This common market idea was a super success. Come the autumn I took weekly space in Dunstable Market. Kemble Pianos had just imported the Yamaha range and we were the first agent in Beds and Bucks. We shifted these organs so fast, brand 'H' haunted me no more.

When Margaret married, her sister Hilary helped out with 'Fly me to the moon' - the only piece she could play - demonstrating and selling a large classical organ. Bourdon, Geigen and Diapason are hardly stops associated with this melody, but she clinched the sale!

As for me, Danarm chainsaws had long since deadened my fingers, one of which I cut to the bone the day I was loaning an organ to Limbury Baptist Church for a carol service. Helen and the girls loaded, to avoid disappointing the young organist, Norman Gurney. A gifted man, who takes the Albert Hall beast in his stride, as well as me, as my publisher.

A rare dream machine was offered me - an ex 'North Sea Gas conversion' mobile showroom. An AEC Mercury artic and 25 foot trailer with generator, kitchen, office, lights, awning steps, enough room to give a small concert and going for a song! A lick of paint and lettering, and the world of organs would be my oyster! Sadly, no way would this outfit turn into my yard, or be accepted in the market. The cost of shortening the trailer was prohibitive. What a waggon! What a dream!

After nine years we got out of the organ 'rat race' as we had got in - at the right time. Much is said about the therapy of music. Indeed it soothes the savage breast. In 1985, housebound, and depressed from cardiac problems, an old friend, Clive Hawes, introduced me to organ recordist Bill Ravenall, who kept me in tapes to work out my aggression and throw off my malaise. One tape he sent was 'Bideford Quay', a rousing march composed at this favourite place of the late Armsbee Bancroft, and played by him on his beloved Burton on Trent WurliTzer, from which he entertained thousands live, and via the radio. The Town Clerk of Bideford heard and arranged for the sole rights to the march, now frequently played by their Band. Armsbee, a Methodist Church Organist for 35 years, from the age of 13, would include his own arrangement of a hymn in his Sunday concerts.

About 500 people attended his memorial service, which speaks volumes for this Evangelist of the console.

A prolonged flow of happy music does more to brace up the spirits than any other influence. Try it, and see for yourself.

I chainsaw sculptured this organ console from a solid elm trunk. It was better than £££s of advertising for us.

My daughter Margaret.

Hilary, one of the twins.

The Van Urk DAF mobile showroom. We never looked back after this idea. Photograph courtesy of Aza Teeuwen of J. Van Urk.

We called this show 'A Night to Remember', and it was. An organ blew up on Len Rawle (right), next to me, family and friends.

Len Rawle launched our mobile studio, with generator at a steam rally.
'We predominate in the right way'. This Van Urk slogan became ours.

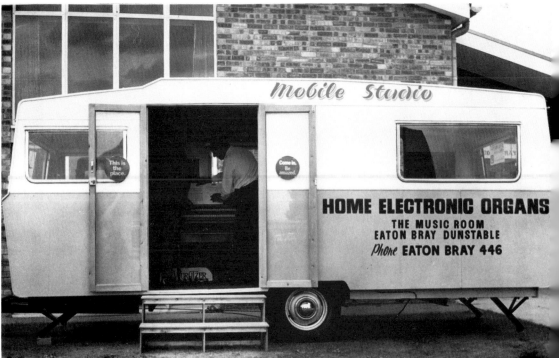

THIRTY TONS
OF MOBILE MUSIC

Appropriately, Reginald Foort was born at Daventry in 1894 beneath the shadow of the massive steel towers which were to transmit his musical brilliance across the world. His father was a church organist and had a music shop in the High Street. Even today, the odd piano bearing the 'Foort' name can be found. At seven years Reg's fingers rippled over the shop pianos with infant dexterity. Aged eleven, he volunteered to play the school organ in the music master's absence. The Royal College of Music and his F.R.C.O. were just natural progressions. As a Naval Officer (1914-19) his cheery pianistics were ever in demand aboard H.M.S. Roberts. When stationed at Gorleston he regularly deputised for a young organist, Mary Cadbury, who was to appear with him quite by chance twenty years later. After the war Reg held several church organist appointments in London. Now previous to this an extraordinary musician named Robert Hope-Jones became an assistant church organist - aged nine. His flair for organs and his job, a telephone engineer, led to a new concept of electric action in organs. His first test detached console was in a churchyard among the tombstones. Bursting with inventive ideas, if not a sense of business, he went to America. He built several advanced designed organs calling them 'one man orchestras'. The WurliTzer Company, then not into keyboard organs, were quick to see the potential, and Robert's cash flow problems. In no time he was glad of a job with them, which accounts for the telephone technology found in these organs.

In 1925 the first WurliTzer crossed the Atlantic, and life for Reginald Foort and his contemporaries was never to be the same. Here was an entertainment organ with fantastic voice ranges, responding to every type of playing. Special effects made it ideal to accompany silent films. An organist rising from the depths, playing his own signature tune, became a major entertainment feature. R.H.J's re-imported musical ideas 'took off'. WurliTzer made a tremendous debut in Foort's hands as organist at the New Gallery Kinema, London, in 1926. In weeks he was broadcasting and recording, albeit via a microphone beside a standard G.P.O. telephone to the Gramophone Company. No Telecom cock-ups in those days! In fact, he recorded a Bournemouth organ via trunk lines many times. His recording of 'In a Monastery Garden' topped any other record sold up to that time. Under the name 'Michael Cheshire' Woolworths sold half a million small records in two weeks - price six pence each, whilst H.M.V. moved three and a quarter million.

The B.B.C. installed their own big British Compton organ in St. George's Hall, London.

Three top organists and Reg opened it in 1936. The programme over-ran. Reg, last on, had his stint cut. Even so, he was appointed staff organist from 350 applicants. When Jack Hylton's band were unable to broadcast, Reg filled the breach for an hour, at short notice, justifying this organ that very night. A 'Daily Express' Gallup Poll on sixty top broadcasters brought Reg twice as many votes as number two, Gracie Fields. Foort was a born communicator, and not just a brilliant organist. Fan mail became a burden to the B.B.C. A chance remark about his garden-less flat during a programme featuring 'flower names' brought floral tributes from ladies all over the U.K. by the van load. In their day the Beatles had nothing on Reg in his. In two years he had made 405 broadcasts - during his B.B.C. career these totalled 1800 in all - and moved into prime listening time. Despite these accolades, vaudeville was prospering, and Reg yearned to meet his public. The idea of a gigantic touring organ was envisaged.

Overtures were made to Reginald Mills, and dance band leader, Marius Winter, forming the Company F.M.W. Limited. Reg wanted an organ that sounded and looked gigantic. The world's biggest organ builders, the Moller Company U.S.A., undertook this colossal task. Its measurements were 42 feet wide, 18 feet high and 15 feet deep. 259 stops controlled 2,370 pipes in 27 ranks, played from a 5-manual console, voiced to Reg's own specification, and the price?: £10,000 ex works in 1938 - 30 tons the lot.

The organ, in 12 sections, was mounted on castors, the heaviest being the $2\frac{1}{2}$ ton relay bank units. It all came over in 65 packing cases on the 'Aquitania'.

Four 16 foot Wheelbase Commer Vans 26 feet long, 13 feet high, were waiting at Southampton. Normand Ltd, Park Royal, London, built these special bodies with steel ramps and hand winches that anchored up front and stowed beside the chassis. Reg specified to Rootes a touring capability of the U.K., Europe, and the U.S.A. Later a smaller Commer was added to facilitate quicker loading. The impressive touring convoy of seven vehicles included Reg's Mercedes Motor Van, and a Commer Minibus for the fifteen staff -drivers cum organ builders, electricians, stage riggers etc. A team of men committed to work together, round the clock. The organ was rushed late to Drury Lane, unpacked, and erected on the world's largest stage. Sandy Macpherson, Foort's eventual successor, was filmed dedicating it at a huge press party, then it was one mad 186 mile dash to Manchester.

Historians have written how, at the outbreak of war, Sandy Macpherson slept and lived with the B.B.C. Compton, playing it for hours on end as a national morale booster, until it was gutted by fire.

Reg opened on time - just - without a practice. The operative word 'Gigantic' defines every facet of the idea. Finance, thinking, transportation, calibre of the team, as well as artist and organ. They played packed houses, to people assured of peace but preparing for gathering war clouds. The Moller music began and ended with 'Keep Smiling', a near impossible command in 1939.

The organ only stopped once. Tommy Trinder had arranged for the power to be cut, then walked on stage with a handle saying - 'He was tired of pumping for Reg', who took it all in good part. One near go was when the 16 inch 25 lbs pressure wind trunk pipe came loose and was held until the interval by two men, one jammed against the wall, his feet in the other's back. In spite of ear plugs it was audio hell back stage. The biggest panic was at Edinburgh, when a driver spotted the $1\frac{1}{4}$ ton console drifting toward the orchestra pit, rushed on and blocked the castors as Reg played on. They played 118 theatres and erected the organ 167 times. There was up to 300 miles between locations, working through Saturday nights, travelling Sundays, erecting, testing, and tuning, for Monday evening. Two of the Commers were caught in a 16 foot snow drift in March 1940, and in the Liverpool blitz one of the staff climbed a cat walk and dealt with three fire bombs 60 feet above the organ.

I never succeeded in locating any of the old drivers, but then found I had sat a row behind one of the team at a St. Albans concert! Wally Street was a fund of information. It seems Reg had a 'Barrie Manilow' effect on housewives, who mobbed him frequently. At the Empire, Middlesbrough, a young lad, Laurie Morley, was shown round the works and given a signed 'photo he has to this day, and it is from him I have learned so much of the Foort story.

A tumultuous reception awaited Reg back home in the New Theatre, Northampton. Arthur Mulliner's garage laid on a fleet of cars and Daventry went mad about their local lad.

Although by now two of the big Commers were commandeered by the R.A.F., Reg kept going, sending half the organ by rail. Sadly the last show was in Cardiff, early 1940. Reg gathered the lads and thanked them with a £50 bonus each.

F.M.W. Limited had no choice. Transport was now impossible. The B.B.C. bought the organ for a pittance, and Sandy broadcast the Moller, which later was installed in London.

Reg toured and played across the U.S.A., where he stayed on in the 1950s. He played his farewell public concert in Vancouver B.C. Canada in 1977 - a programme of all the music that had endeared him to his public worldwide. He loved Finlandia, with which he would end, but this day he closed with 'Land of Hope and Glory' which the great audience sang with him. The applause was tumultuous!

As for the Moller, yet another move awaited it to its final home in the vast auditorium of the Civic Centre, Pasadena, U.S.A. In a letter to my friend Laurie Morley, Doris Stovall, the auditorium manager writes "Mr. Foort was at the dedication concert in 1980 and was pleased his pride and joy had found its perfect home".

Only weeks later Reg passed away. Daventry's famous son has gone, but his gigantic dream lives on and sounds as good as ever.

A POSTSCRIPT

In the autumn of 1939 an excited young eighteen year old lad with four months' experience at the Cinema Organ completed his performance at the Majestic Theatre in Rochester, Kent. His manager had arranged for him to attend the nearby Theatre Royal and be introduced to the sensational Reginald Foort. Back stage, this most affable man, whose show had thrilled the boy so, said "Come on then, I know you want to try out my Moller". Faced with the giant console, five manuals, and row upon row of stops, brought a gasp as Reg gave a brief demonstration, then handed over to the youth. Commencing with 'Nola' he played for an hour until midnight. The kind and helpful master of the key board was most generous with his time and knowledge.

Fifty years on, George Blackmore (for that was the young man's name) remembers that night vividly. Little did George know he was destined to broadcast the Moller in 1948 on the B.B.C., with repeat invites throughout the 1950s. In fact in 1962 he broadcast the

116 Moller more than any other organist, thirty times - and logged over eighty, before the final broadcast from the Moller in October 1963.

When the Moller was sold and shipped to Holland, George was invited over to Hilversum to record three programmes, before it was sold again after the death of the resident organist, Cor Steyn.

Back in the U.S.A. the Moller Company rebuilt the organ in a San Diego Pizza Parlour. Reginald Foort did the opening honours in 1975. In 1976 George was invited to cross the Atlantic to record an L.P. 'The Magnificent Moller, thus becoming the only organist to play the Moller in all three countries. 'Moller, Foort and Blackmore', three great names, inseparably linked.

The fleet of Commers Reginald Foort specified to tour the UK, Europe and the USA. Photograph courtesy of Harvey Roehl, USA.

When joined by the other three vehicles, this was a most impressive convoy indeed. Photograph courtesy of Harvey Rouhl, USA.

The signed photograph Reg gave Laurie Morley at the Empire Theatre, Middlesborough.

The cover of a souvenir programme sent me from Norfolk. This Foort smile did so much for sponsors Macleans Toothpaste.

CHARLIE AND TIM

Legend has it that George Blackmore had brought the organ up at the end of 'Gaumont British News' so many times that big letters 'G.B.' was faded into the back of his coat. Well whatever, they queued in the rain, and stood at the back as the 'Radetsky March' came over like old times in February, 1989, at the St. Albans Organ Museum.

From boyhood, fairgrounds held a magnetic attraction for Charles Hart. World War Two had stopped this successful St. Albans builder and brought enforced holidays at home for all. It is not therefore unexpected to find this man erecting a few children's amusements by the lake in the local park in 1939. A handful of girls and fellows were charismatically drawn and helped run this venture. This enterprise ran until 1973 when Charles was just no longer fit enough to hump three massive mechanical organs and other leisure paraphernalia back and forth each summer.

Charles got into amusement buying, selling, and hiring, which led to his great love of mechanical organs. When he heard of Belgium Cafe and Dance Hall voiced instruments being scrapped in the 1960s, he commenced trips with his lorry and rescued over thirty in all. Indulging his hobby, a growing number of visitors seemed willing to scramble over builder's yard materials to hear these gems of yester-year. Charles' hospitable wife, Tim, made cups of tea, and the embryo of a most exceptional working music museum had taken form. Buildings improved but enthusiasts still had to cope with job lots of dolls to dog baskets, this wheeler-dealer would buy. In 1980 Mr. and Mrs. Hart opened the present building they had financed to house the jewels of their collection, music boxes, organettes, upright and grand player pianos, one an extremely rare Welte, as is a Moller 'Artiste' organ roll player. Musical science years ahead of its time!

Volunteers, adhering to the Master, did much of the building. Stories abound of raising a thirty foot R.S.J. by hand, holding down roofing in a gale etc. These exploits are endless.

Dilapidated instruments are lovingly restored, and much more is effected by the great un-named 'Tuesday Nighters', a working party that includes parents, wives, girl and boy friends. One, albeit a twenty-three year old, had attended twenty years. A great camaraderie blossoms 'midst the soldering and dull laborious tasks'. In 1978 Charles set up a charitable trust to perpetuate the 'Hart Vision'. With great wisdom he chose four men, who are more like disciples than trustees, to manage this palace of pioneers of early music. Eric Cockayne, who has written a most authoritative book on mechanical organs; Keith Pinner, Sales

Officer and gifted in punching out new cardboard books of organ music; Peter Allen, Society Treasurer, and player piano enthusiast; finally Chairman Bill Walker, whose memories of the Harts border on the sacred. Here is a man who seems to unlock everything from the gates to his sophisticated recording gear, accounting for audio souvenirs of one's visit, available from the shop. Goodies, unavailable elsewhere, often come from enthusiasts around the world, and are sold in the Museum Shop to help defray running costs.

Each Sunday afternoon the public enjoy a conducted tour of the instruments played in turn. This includes a session on a gorgeous little 'Rutt' theatre organ, used also for monthly concerts. The tradition of the biscuit and cup of free Hart tea lives on. Charles' greatest coup was surely the rescue of the fine WurliTzer Organ from the Granada Edmonton, London, in 1969. Organist Bernard Wooster (25 years with Granada), tipped Charles of the pending 'wreckers ball'. Miraculously, this 6 ton organ of some 900 pipes was removed in seven days by Hart-inspired volunteers, working nights, fed by Tim from her bubble car. Fearing the scrap man's beady eye, Charle slept beside his leaden treasures one night. This great crown of the Hart musical jewels soon will speak again in all its glory, thanks to Tuesday night intensive care.

An air of warm welcome pervades here. Commitment appears like a cult or religion for some. Time and again they describe Mr. and Mrs. Hart in two words, 'generous' and 'kind'! Worthy praise of a couple who come over like practical Christians, not linked to a church, yet they were founder members of the local Christadelphian movement, whose ideas on Sunday observance later clashed with those of Charles. The Harts had no children, or did they? Tim was a genius at short notice feeding, when perhaps a dozen or more famished young faces appeared at the table. It strikes me the couple lived well below their means, with unusual standards of luxury. Their 'Mercedes' took the form of a 97 key magnificent Mortier Organ. A 95 key Bursens Cafe Organ was their boat. The 121 key DeCap Dance Organ was preferred to a desirable cottage. The 92 DeCap Dance Organ 'Jeannake' would have priority over any jacuzzi, and the Steinway to a swimming pool. To set up such a trust is not uncommon, but nowhere else will one find such a collection of nostalgic melody makers, administered by devotees, who have so captured, and held, the 'Hart' dream, that this man and woman live on. Charles Hart amassed a vast fortune, and all of us were remembered in his will.

"Spread a little Happiness" was not just his favourite song, it was his gospel. He believed it, he lived it. What a remarkable couple!!

120

*Charles Hart with
his Leyland Organ
van.*

*Charlie took this
Bedford and
trailer many times
to Belgium to
rescue organs. He
tended to be
oblivious to
Customs officials,
whom he disliked.*

*The St.Albans Organ Museum.
The Trustees (left to right):
Eric Cockayne, Bill Walker,
Peter Allen and Keith Pinner.*

WARTIME MEMORIES

In 1939, our village of Eaton Bray went on to a wartime footing. I joined the Auxiliary Fire Service in a shed at the rear of the Chequers Inn. Fire fighting could be thirsty work! We were issued with uniforms, and a well worn 14.9 H.P. Ford car, never intended to tow a trailer pump, and carry six hefty firemen, who helped to push it up every hill for miles around. Down hill was better, but not for a hen in the road that flew up, and was found trapped unharmed between the headlight and radiator miles later back at the Chequers. One night, at the height of the London Blitz, 250 acres of timber were on fire in Surrey Docks - "Send every pump you have, the whole bloody world is on fire" came the message. (That night parched firemen drank from the Thames). As I was baking potatoes and our driver, George Brinklow, was well into ale and dominoes next door, a V.I.P. Fire Chief called to say we were on red alert for London. "Don't talk so daft" said George. "I have to adjust the clutch every 10 miles now. How will this man and his mates fight fires, after pushing this lot 30 miles" he exploded, kicking a wheel. "If you are sent, you will go" insisted the V.I.P. Thankfully for us, and London, we never were.

If this sounds like "Dad's Army", it was, but had nothing on the Home Guard up the 'Comp'. Under Mr. Danvers (a kind of Captain Mainwaring), their well intended antics were hilarious. An instructor, of all people, fired a live round that went through a wall and two cars outside. Nervous Alfie Skeggs fired one through a ceiling, and tried to deny it, as smoke poured from his rifle. Charlie Stokes got himself a sword, challenged a horse in darkness, and got kicked where it hurt most. Alec Jackson fitted cycle wheels to a grenade thrower that looked like a baby cannon. At practice, a wooden projectile went through the the Captain's legs. The Quartermaster cared for the lads' beer during an exercise and was found blind drunk on their return. Again in darkness, Fred Lugsden was ordered to hold bushes aside for Mr. Danvers, enabling him to plunge unknowingly headlong into the river. Our trigger-happy lads peppered a British cannister with shot as it dropped by parachute. Captain 'D' refused Loll Piggott's request for petrol coupons before a journey. When stranded in the wilds he handed them over. These were promptly placed in the tank to prove a car runs on petrol, not paper.

Another hilarious incident occurred when our Home Guard infiltrated Studham platoon canteen: they were recognised by a young lady server who explained: Here is the enemy - charge them for their tea".

Dad' Army, our illustrious Home Guard. On an excercise some of these men infiltrated Studham's platoon canteen. A lady server recognized a lad who was courting a local girl and shouted "They are the enemy – make them pay for their tea".

Thankfully, the Germans never invaded.

My brother married, and took a derelict farm at Pulloxhill. A contractor, Harry Rook, was ploughing over hundreds of ant hills with a Fordson, ancient even in 1940. I was astonished to see a magneto on a crude frame driven by a sloppy made up chain, that replaced the coil box. This uneducated little cripple, who reeked of shag and oil, said "Fords say that won't work, but she is easy to 'time', besides no German will ever start her. I take the mag. home each night". The law required unattended vehicles to be immobilised during the war.

Harry lived alone in a caravan surrounded with antiquated implements. He used a great International Mogul for big jobs. He seemed to have it on permanent demonstration, since he could start it, and the Dealer couldn't. Field service was via a 4 x 4 Pony and cart he had mounted on a Morris axle, to carry his T.V.O. oil and tools. Outside his van an old hen scratched with a wooden leg. "She lost her leg in a mower. I cut that peg and taped it on. She lays well, so she must be happy" he said, beaming through his grime. So was Harry, contented with his simple lot, typical of thousands of his kind, who fed us in the war.

One Sussex Downs' area became a 400 acre field, harvested by 15 Fordson's binders and 30 Land Army girls: typical of the war effort.

Remember organic farming couldn't feed us all then. Could it now?

I JOIN THE ARMY

My first orders in the Royal Engineers were over my bunk.

They read - 'Beds will be made up, as laid down, in standing orders'. The Army was like that!

My driving test on a 6 x 4 AEC Marshall Bridging waggon was a cinch. Then a short four-wheeled folding boat trailer was attached to this longish vehicle, and my efforts to reverse it had a group of A.T.S. drivers in hysterics! One's compassion led her to hop up and share the unruly wheel with me. Our faces almost touched as we scanned through the rear window. Her perfume played havoc with my concentration, and ego!

This was Irene, who was a virtuoso of the Dennis gearbox, so rightly named 'The Pig'. Irene was quite a girl!

I drove my first Army vehicle on the road as duty driver at a moment's notice. It was a loaded Bedford Q.L. 4 x 4 Troop Carrier, with extended chassis, to seat 29 persons. A notice inside warned 'All personnel will remain seated whilst in transit'. At a 'T' junction, three Land Girls in shorts, with ample thighs, were hoeing, backs to the road. I changed down to turn, someone 'wolf whistled', the ensuing rush to the rear had me across the road, and into the ditch. After a few choice words from the Officer, the lads assisted recovery. He then turned on me with "and you are not without blame, these chaps are not made of wood, you know; you saw those girls, where's your anticipation, man"?

Our destination was at an outbreak of Foot and Mouth Disease. The working party were burying the remains of a dairy herd and as the last burnt carcass was pushed in with one of our Cat. D.4s, some of the lads had to restrain the farmer from jumping in and perishing with his life's work.

I have written elsewhere about my adventures during two years driving the Major who led a small team of men that tested earth moving equipment, mostly for 'D' Day.

The principal project was trials on Britain's first Tank Dozer. We were like civilians in uniform, no parades, just a normal 16 hour day instead. Two lads, Jack Sampson and Bert Kreft, had the job of testing a newly captured German $3/4$ track 18 ton Famo mobile slewing crane. It had a telescopic jib with a 10 ton lift, and manual stabilisers. In fact, it was far superior to anything similar on tracks in the U.K. Our boffin's answer to this was to mount a 10 ton Coles Crane on the front of a Churchill. At the official demonstration, all their sums were proved wrong, when Bert brought this 38 ton tank right onto its nose, attempting to lift 7 tons. When some idiot Brass Hat said "now travel forward", Bert dropped the load with exasperation!

One of the best kept secrets of the war was that an armoured Cat. D.7 was tracked to a nearby farm after dark. Here a dense long hedge, and all trees therein, were dozed out in the moonlight, for a farmer. There were no military reasons behind the exercise, and the delighted farmer financed a kind of indefinite standing order at the local, for all the beer the lads could drink, which in Tom Nicholls' case was quite considerable. I remember Jack Sampson best as the man who went Christmas shopping in Winchester with a Scammell and D.8 behind. As for Bert Kreft, he heard the only way to be posted from the dreaded Tetbury Camp was to dance with the Sgt. Major's girlfriend at the weekly hop. Bert couldn't dance, but after a couple of drinks, and about five steps with the lass, he was posted the following Monday!

One morning we had been delayed at Barnes, and as I raced up the long drive I learned we had half an hour to get to Harefield for a Ministry Meeting. Traffic was bad but out on the A40 I really got going! This road was notoriously littered with service staff cars, ferrying War Lords and V.I.P.s to and from Northolt Aerodrome. Some I passed and some I couldn't.

Those cars were mostly Humber limousines (Pullmans), and one such vehicle was hogging both lanes ahead, its speed too slow to follow, but too fast to pass. Squeezing in between the central reservation, I changed down, took the Morris Utility up to peak revs and hooted as we pushed through. The Major looked up from the sheets of reports that always occupied him in transit and spotted the occupant of the limo and exploded - "My God, it's Churchill". By now both vehicles were about to go onto a roundabout, neck and neck. Realising Mr C's contribution to the War effort could be as important as ours, I gave way as we each swerved onto the roundabout. This required my size tens, hard on the brake, which brought a whole avalanche of kit about both of us. The Major was entombed in drums of oil, and a few of the spare crawler track plate pads I carried with me. Churchill never mentioned the incident in his wartime memories, so I put it in mine!

During World War Two not all mass evacuations concerned children.

When the guns were sent south, the order came to move 60,000 ewes and lambs from off Romney Marshes in two weeks. A fleet of mostly double deck cattle trucks, with lambs above their mothers, transported 100,000 animals in 1,000 lorry loads. The reception areas included Beds and Bucks. In all that number there were only six casualties. Yet another lesser known transport achievement.

Hall and Company Limited of Croydon were chosen to co-ordinate and deliver vast quantities of aggregate to the South Coast Ports for the Mulberry Harbours' construction. The Ministry demanded 4,000 tons of ballast seven days a week for 150 days. Churchill gave top priority to 150 tippers that averaged 60 miles, from quarry to dock, and covered 2,250,000 miles between them.

Many a bleary-eyed driver stuck a 90 hour week for the whole five months. I heard that as one exhausted driver fell out of the Cab, another climbed in without stopping the engine.

Hall had 700 vehicles, 350 of which were Bedford. One 3 tonner was still going strong after 700,000 miles.

I traced 85 year old Thomas Hobbs. He worked a 14 hour day 7 days a week for 3 months; then the Ministry gave him a Sunday off. He was doing five trips a day from Chichester, or Midhurst, or even Kent to Southampton, or Portsmouth dockyards.

If the sirens went whilst unloading, the gates were locked, and time had to be made up on the road. The worst aspects were the blackout, the hunger, and not being able to tell the wife about the job. Tom paid tribute to his old Bedford, and said "We survived, thousands were not so lucky".

Needless to say Hall delivered on schedule.

'Phoenix', 'Bombardon', and 'Whale' were the enigmatic code names given to gigantic concrete caissons, 200 feet long, 56 feet wide, and 60 feet high, the creation of 20,000 Civil Engineering workers.

Secrecy was such that even as they were towed across the channel, few people knew their proposed use.

The reinforcing girder bays, 36 feet long, 11 feet wide, weighing 12 tons, were a bit much for every 24ft flat bed lorry available in the U.K.

Those bound for Stranraer knew all about crossing Shap in January - fog, ice, and snow. The blitz was endured in matchboard cabs, without tin hats. Metal cabs and convoy cover, enjoyed by service vehicles, were not for these men. Surely they were "Lorry Drivers of the Year" for six years.

Bert and Sam (centre) had to test this 'Famo' captured $^3/4$ track crane for the War Office. A 450 volt dynamo in the chassis powered the crane from a radial engine. On an 80 mile road trial, a steering fault reduced one lock by half. Tired of shunting on corners, they drove over roundabouts by the dozen!

June 1987. Left to right: Ex cpl. Tom Nicholls, ex Major Lachie Sturrock, ex Captain Dudley Simmons, Bert Kreft and myself gather round John Marchant's Centaur Tank Dozer to launch my Muck Shifting book. Photograph courtesy of the Leighton Buzzard Observer

NELLIE

A man named Ted Holmes was the only person who remembered 'Nellie'. I was enquiring around the village of Lilley, near Hitchin, Herts. No, not an old girl friend! 'Nellie' was the code name given to a trench cutting machine of elephantine proportions.

In the early part of the war Churchill instructed model makers Bassett Lowke to produce a working model of a tank-like tracked machine. Finally, the dimensions were 75 feet long, 18 feet wide, 10 feet high, weighing 125 tons and powered by 1,200 h.p. Ruston Bucyrus engines. This Lincoln based firm was assisted by 350 other companies. A giant plough up front pushed 'Nellie' into the ground, as rotary cutters discharged earth onto side conveyors. One prototype was tested by Royal Engineer muck shifting units in Clumber Park, Notts, and the other at Lilley Hoo, in 1943.

Ted Holmes was in the Observer Corps, but recalls only heavily armed guards, the roar of the engines, and a man killed when 'Nellie' struck a power line. The last thing the War Office considered was the logistics problem! As I have said, the Army was like that. How do you inconspicuously transport to the Siegfried line a machine broken down onto three 50 ton trailers, pulled and pushed by five tractors each, at 4 m.p.h.?

Consequently, 'Nellie' never got either off the ground or rather into it. One of these machines was still around in the 1950s. We have seen some amazing adaptations, but it would have taken a most inventive Timberman to find a job for a machine that had a turning circle of one mile!

TRACTOR - AEC - 4 X 4 MEDIUM ARTILLERY

At the end of the African campaign the AEC Matador received official commendation of being the best medium class tractor in either opposing armies.

Many associate chartered accountant, Kenneth Rankin, with 35 years of environmental friendly 'Green' service to post-war Britain; the man, who in the 1960s raised by his own efforts the money for Eskdalemuir Forest, 36,000 acres of proof that landscape, wildlife, and a living for village communities can be the result of modern forestry; the man who, at 80, still pleads the cause of forestry to every Government, regardless of colour. Fewer will know of his exploits with Matadors or of his experiences in war. Kenneth Rankin, Captain R.A.(Retired), kept and published later a diary throughout the siege of Tobruk - called "Top-Hats in Tobruk". This siege, the longest in British military history, lasted 242 days and thus prevented defeat in the Middle East war in 1941. He wrote not only of his depressions and fears but also of his strong faith in God.

After a German counter attack, 15-ton guns swung on Matadors, loaded with ammunition, 14 men, all their kit, food, and loot, as they raced 200 miles back to Tobruk. The Matadors had their governors removed, giving speeds up to 50 m.p.h. across the desert, through blown up passes, and on rough terrain. The Gunners had perfect confidence in their Mats., and their ex London Transport Drivers and Mechanics. Over 9,000 M.A.T.S. (Medium Artillery Tractors), served in every theatre of war.

Hundreds of tributes were received by AEC. One told of a hasty retreat, when a Matador, carrying a Jeep, and towing a 4 x 4, 3 tonner, came upon a 6 x 6 Re-fueler with a burnt-out clutch, from towing another 6 x 6 Tanker. The two 6 x 6 vehicles were tow-barred together, to the rear of the 4 x 4, and that old Mat. towed all three for 50 miles up mountain

THE FASTEST MATADOR IN THE WEST

"Matador" - 'A performer whose task is to fight and kill.' The Oxford Dictionary.

George Croasdale's Matador UUE 106G (MMM, page 51) re-engined with a Perkins 6354, has stood up well to the doubling of her revs! However, a run from Stratford-on-Avon to Windermere in 4 $\frac{1}{4}$ hours did bring the transfer box oil to the boil, but removing the front prop shaft overcame this!

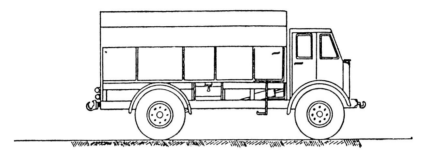

JOHN MARCHANT'S ARMY

A cross section of over 50 ex military vehicles awaited me at Furtho Pit, near Milton Keynes, when I visited for tree work in 1974. John Marchant differs from other collectors, in that as a Contractor, he has worked many of his vehicles at sometime or another. Starting with a £15 untaxed Lloyd Bren Carrier in 1947 (new ones were £40), the carrier was towed home, in theory at least, on a rigid bar behind John's Morris 8. However, I have a feeling more pushing than pulling was done!

His love affair with Canadian vehicles began in 1948, when a Ford three tonner, price £17.50, proved capable of carrying 7 tons of corn.

An ex R.A.F. Fordson Roadless half track ploughed some 3,000 hours, and an Allis Chalmers H.D. 7 W Bulldozer slogged year in year out in the Marchant hands.

Restoring and rallying a 'Daimler Dingo' armoured car today is acceptable. In 1972, with son and daughter as "Commanders", it was certifiable!

John took the family on the first 'D' Day rally to Normandy.

His daughter, Janet, drove her amateur rebuilt Jeep 700-odd miles across Europe in 1978, proving the symptom is a genetical one!

Most astounding of all was John's ex scrap yard 'Centaur' Tank Dozer. His idea of restoring and dieselising it sounded a bit fanciful. That day two seeds germinated, one within him, that he would do just that, and one within me, that I would endeavour to trace the men who had developed it, and write up their story.* It took us both 13 years to do it.

To transform this 26 tons of solid track seized rusted armour, that last ran in 1959, is a feat that would have kept the 'Bovington Boys' busy. To replace the 400 h.p. V.12 Liberty engine that could guzzle 12 gallons of petrol an hour with a Detroit V.6. two stroke diesel,

---

*"Muck Shifting for King George", now out of print.

was sheer dogged enthusiasm.

Bert Kreft attended the conversion tests, and was most impressed.

The War Office designated this Tank Dozer the 'Trailblazer'. An apt name also for this oily overalled top military vehicle historian and author, who has 'blazed a trail' of military vehicle history across the world for over 40 years.

John Marchant at work with 03CY26,
his Vickers Armstrong 240 hp 'Vigor'.
Imagine his delight to find this actual
tractor featured in the W.D. handbook.

RECOVERY

Since they both require power winches, recovery and timber haulage are close allies. Prior to this, a hefty team of farm or timber horses would be called upon to remove early vehicles from undignified positions.

In the early 1920s, my father was collecting eggs in Tilsworth. The mare, harnessed to a four wheeled van, grazed the verge by the pond, when the whole lot overturned into deep water. Some eggs were salvaged via a long ladder before numerous farm horses extracted the wreckage.

Today, Eaton Bray boasts umpteen wrecker trucks. Ian and Sylvia Dominey have long since sold their ex U.S.A. Brockway 6 x 6, now replaced by a bonneted Scania Vabis.

Ian learned his craft from a chainsmoker, who converted mileage to 'ciggies' saying - 'this job is about 5, 10, or 15 'fags' from here'. Sylvia has about four years' action behind her. Mostly with her Crew Cab Transit and 4 ton winch. From the old M1 to the new M25, this lass is a credit to her profession.

Of garages, it took me 10 years to realise I was paying over £1 an hour extra van service to wait in a Dealer's armchair, watching colour T.V. Next door to Ian, Barry Cato displays no Works Course Certificates: just a calendar of a lady accidentally photographed adjusting her 'bra'. His service is second to none!

I am ever indebted to the Potton family, whose 'mighty Antar' graced the cover of my last book.

The publicity gained for CORDA from the four page spread in 'Truck and Driver' magazine was inestimable.

For most of a day Tony Potton had poured enough petrol into the 18 litre, 250 b.h.p. engine for 'photo shots and test drives, whilst wife Linda poured coffee into top vehicle journalist Nick Baldwin's entourage.

The Antar had consumed 73 gallons of petrol, being driven up from John Cooper's at Worthing. Linda followed with their American Ford Thunderbird, which I imagine was only a little less thirsty! Matthew, the elder son, is dedicated to the Antar. With parents on holiday, and aged only 20, in sole charge, he was called out to a six wheeled Leyland 'Bison' loaded skip lorry that had plunged 20 feet down a bank off the A5. This indeed was a job for the 25 ton Antar, whose 10ft 3inch width required Police dispensation on the highway. Matthew got an H.G.V. licence holder to drive to the scene, then took over and recovered the 'Bison', with all the skill he had learned from Tony.

As for younger brother, Simon, he frequently flashes me from one of the eight "Go Getters" in the T.P. fleet, all under radio control from base by Linda.

Just after the Lockerbie incident, our village was aroused one night by an oncoming roar, reaching its peak near my home. For my benefit, three loud blasts on the Antar's trumpet horns sounded.

A Foden eight wheeler, loaded with chalk, had left the road, run through a wall, and stopped short of a house. This massive load, grossing over 30 tons on suspended tow, had split the silencer, hence the decibels of a Jumbo Jet.

Recovery folk are the hairy chested section of the winching fraternity. (No, not you, Sylvia.) Blood, as well as being always on call, is an additional hazard. Timbermen are never called upon to deal with a driver's head rolling around on the back seat! Tony Potton has!!!

Having featured a 1914 ex Army Mule elsewhere, what about the very latest ex W.D. vehicles around.

John Cooper's normal forestry contracting business in Worthing has an interesting diversification.

John was called upon to recover bogged down plant so many times, he now has a specialist fleet of vehicles doing just this, right along the south coast. Oldest and smallest is his 1945 Matador. Two big sisters come next, a couple of AEC Militants, a Mk. I, now equipped with a telescopic crane, and 20 ton hydraulic winch. The other is a Mk. 3, 6 x 6 on 1600 x 20 tyres, with air operated 15 ton winch, anchor, slewing crane, and power steering. Her AEC AV760 14 litre engine is good for 55 m.p.h. on the road. A recent acquisition is a 1983 Foden, FH70, 6 x 6 gun tractor, with a 5 ton Atlas crane, a 12 ton hydraulic winch up front, and a 40 ton one at the rear. With three P.T.O.s, diff. locks, and cross diff. locks, high and low range, coming from a 305 h.p. Rolls Royce turbo charged 'power house', this is a superb piece of kit, and one of two sold off by the Army. Even so, pride of the fleet is John's 6 x 4 Mk. 3. Thornycroft 'Antar' Rolls Royce straight 8, super charged, with a 50 ton Turner winch, and John's own hydraulic anchor, still bearing the Royal Engineers' Badge, I'm thrilled to note. The Antar occasionally works in timber, as did John's former Mark I Antar, that featured on the cover of MMM. None of your buying half a dozen, and hoping one is a runner, the old 'Ruddington' way in today's circumstances. John's hundreds of photographs have to be seen to be believed. Sea defence plant seems most accident prone, and breaking the suction before the rope or winch is an acquired art. John is often called after 'fools have rushed in'.

Just one incident involved a big excavator, jammed behind a groyne, minus a track, and facing high tide. Already a Diamond 'T' had broken an undersized rope, and without a snatchblock, deserved to. A hefty Scammell didn't want to know. Standing on Hove promenade, this job was a pushover for the Antar. Like all recovery jobs, it's a blending of brain and brawn, perception, and power. Thirty years in timber have given John Cooper these qualities.

Ian and Sylvia's old 6 x 6 ex USA Brockway, scrapped and now believed restored.

Matthew, now with his HGV licence, moves the 30 ton loaded Foden on suspended tow. Tony first became acquainted with the Antar by bringing her home through Epsom on Derby Day, 1980.

Would you believe this 1945 Matador winched this bogged excavator clear of quick sands? I didn't until John explained his intricate snatch blocking, and that a Cat D8 held this (now perhaps longer wheelbased) Mat down. It took 6 hours of pulling and resting for suction braking.

John hooked onto the boom – there was nowhere else.

This 70 ton Krupp crane toppled onto a new building. When you are called to a job like this, one doesn't hook on and rev like hell! It's the brain that the recovery man puts in bottom gear!

This ex W.D. Foden gets where John's Antar cannot. Be it the big hurricane-blown tree, the tide-submerged pile driver, the Foden 6 x 6 will get there. In fact they have tried to bog this Foden and can't.

WR U735 Thorneycroft Mighty Antar 6 x 4 with hydraulic anchor. Ex Royal Engineers – need I say more?

Ivan Chant of Frome with his 4 wheel steer Autocar 'Mean Machine' (see chapter one). His photograph album made me gasp, as did the vehicle's price, ex Florida, USA.

MEN AND MOTORS -
EATON BRAY REMEMBERED

I remember, I remember the village where I was born.
The ducks, fruit, and carnations, 'Eclipse' flour milled by Thorne.
'This much sought after village' has changed beyond my dreams.
Today it's all commuters, computers and car phones
And High Street traffic jams it seems.

Remember Kingfishers down the Meads - Nightingales in Harling road - Tadpole field - Paddling in the ford - Meadows golden with buttercups - Slides on Tom Gurney's frozen pond - you do? Well the following pages are dedicated to you.

June 1922 was very hot, and Mother welcomed my birth, a brother for seven year old Eric.

The mostly sixteenth century but part Victorian house where I still live, and hope to die (but not yet) was a bastion of local Methodism. Gifted brothers Gurney once resided here. One was a violinist. The other's artistry is seen in the decorative roll of past vicars in St Mary's Church. Both these men were known for untidiness, a tradition my wife Helen claims, I have maintained.

At school I was nicknamed 'Shusher'! Whilst other lads hitched a lift hanging on the tailboard of Thorne's steam lorry, I wore out my shoes shuffling along beside it hissing imaginary steam, pretending to be both engine and driver. Grandpa Fred Bates owned Moor End Farm before Tom Gurney. The house has changed little outside, and memories of his vast collection of butterflies and stuffed birds in the kitchen still survive. Here was to be my first encounter with death. In 1927, 8 year old Phyllis, daughter of his second marriage, was killed in a road accident, and the gory details, not intended for my ears, haunted me for years.

Grandpa James Sanders was astute in the business of pig and poultry dealing. His three daughters and son contributed much to his success. Grandpa rented, then bought The Lodge, previously the Pedley Estate office, for £860 in 1915. When the family left 65 Moor End (now Denson's Office), Grandma, ever proud of her furniture, requested the horse and waggonette walk past the School. Thus Mrs Paddock, the Head's wife, had a chance to see it. This lady had a Degree in Domestic Science, and ours was the first Elementary School in Bedfordshire to have cookery lessons. It was said her husband, a strict disciplinarian, had scarred inner thighs, where scholars had bitten him as he caned their buttocks, (heads between his legs). The day school was built by the Wesleyans in 1864 and closed in 1988. When my father was called up, his sister Lizzie undertook the hire work with the Landau - weddings and funerals, plus the regular waggonette service to Hemel Hempstead Hospital. Once a local on the way there, in agony from a kidney stone, begged permission to pop behind a hayrick and, after a scream, emerged saying 'turn the horse round - I've passed it'.

My early memories of Grandpa's model 'T' Ford lorry begin with holding the wheel from his lap. I recall his tickling the tremblers on the coil box and the lights that dimmed, as revs dropped on corners. Cyclists he would rebuke for a one arm tailboard tow. Luton tram lines were identical width to the Ford's solid tyres. The lorry could be in great trouble if the rear wheels got stuck in wet tramlines whilst the front wheels were clear - a crab-like stance embarrassing to Grandpa. Regular deliveries of pigs to the Co-op Butchery in High Town required reversing down a narrow alleyway. Grandpa would engage gear as a couple of bloodstained slaughtermen appeared grasping a front wheel each, steering the lorry as it reversed, in return for one or two cracked eggs. This was the going rate for most favours – no one had heard of salmonella then! During the mid 1920s, posters announced Sir Alan Cobham's Air Circus was to visit Billington Road, beside the railway at Leighton Buzzard. Father took us to this spectacular event, but stayed with the mare because of the noise. On our return, he related one of the team had told him the day would come when people would travel in planes, just as they did in the trains passing by.

Long before then, three year old Eddie Impey let a cat out of a bag, running to see Graham Wright in the first plane to pass over here in 1909. Grandpa had two maiden sisters, Temperance and Phoebe, who lived in a lonely cottage a mile outside Northall. The honeysuckle, snowdrops, neat box hedge, the four-poster bed, cats-whisker wireless, and kettle on the hob, leap fresh to mind. The sisters were Sunday School Teachers, Cattle Minders, and Seamstresses, with clients in London. They were most adept with the pitch fork, both in the field and as a means of self protection. In fact when two Italian prisoners-of-war were caught in their hen house, they rounded up the whole gang and held them at fork point, pending police intervention. If these formidable ladies had their time today, I imagine they would be prominent youth workers, into cattle injections, have their own dress-making outlet in Chelsea and be the first 'Guardian Angels' on the Euston Line.

Three local tearaways on motor bikes tried to ride up the steep face of the Orange Pit of the Dunstable Downs, with imaginable results. One was Bob Palmer, another Guss Thorne, and the third, Freddie Hawkins, on his Norton. His days with Costins coaches and lorries were but a step to his own. Freddie had one of the first 4 Studebakers to be imported in 1934-35. The vehicle won great acclaim, transporting everything from flowers to soot. Today his son and grandson are so proud of their current ERFs, they literally fly a Union Jack in the yard. From here 1,400 mile round trip journeys to the Hebrides are a contrast to former haulage. These were not the first waggons to roll from the rear of the old Pub, 'The Labour in Vain' (the sign depicted a woman endeavouring to scrub a black boy white).

Years before, Tom Howe lived here and did the London run with horse and cart. Billy Ellingham, and others in the Rye, a nearby road, loaded 36 trusses of straw - over half a ton. Leaving mid afternoon, the convoy drivers would fill up at the 'Golden Rule' pub at Dagnall, light one or two lanterns, then go on up to the Smoke, as it really was then, through the

Fred Hawkins had one of the first Studebakers imported. Today a fine fleet of ERFs travel the entire UK from a yard that has seen 100 years of transport.

night. Many an old horse knew the way from memory.

Stories abound of these 30 mile each way hauls. One Harry Bliss lost all his hair from laying hours on the manure and soot backloaded from the cab horse stables, some bagged by Eaton Bray women in London. One driver walked back six miles to find his hat in the road. One complained of misleading directions. He had looked out for a Marble Arch that he found wasn't! Some carts passed under a building where hams hung curing. Many mysteriously 'caught up' on the loads. Weighbridge fiddles amounted to a 56lb weight in horses' nose bags. Near Watford the services of an unattended trace horse on a hill were available for three pence, left in a box. The creaking of the returning waggons was accompanied by merry songs, bellowing from the drinkers in the 'Five Bells'. Various ditties were remembered, and sung beautifully by the late Harry Scott. I have a recording of a song he often sang "You never miss the water until the well runs dry". This accounts for the vocal entertainment his son Gaius brought us through the 'Stardusters' concert party, started at the local Methodist church. These horsedrawn waggons would be serviced by the makers, Groom Brothers, at nearby Honeywick. David, the humorous one, claimed the first time he went up a ladder it was down a well!

Up to twenty unemployed farm labourers at a time would congregate at the Blacksmiths seeking casual work, which was described by George Cook, as follows: "About six of us went in carts to harvest a big field at Luton, when Stockingstone Road was a dirt track. By night we lay under a cart sheet 'aside' the rick. By day the sun was so hot margarine in an old cup nearly boiled". Here George was to see the biggest 'Bedfordshire Clanger' of his life. This was a long pastry with meat and vegetables one end and jam the other, calculated to sustain a man in the field.

George continued - "The Boss come on a 'orse' with a big lump of beef in a pail full of gravy, and we cut bits off with a shut knife. It were 1914 - I were 12! - I ploughed and mowed, reaped and sowed, and never missed getting the harvest home for the next 67 years. I've seen 'em' thresh with the flail, steam, and these 'ere' combines".

Stanbridgeford railway station was about 1¼ miles from Eaton Bray. Nearby Totternhoe Knolls, then a tourist attraction, had my aunt, father, and others meet the trippers in with waggonettes. Porter Tom Goodyear took calculated risks, holding the crossing gates for traffic, as trains bore down upon him. Whilst yards away Grandpa would impatiently hoot, skid to a standstill protesting 'you could see me coming Tom', to be told, 'so was the train'!

The first ever demonstration at our W.I. was given by a Stanbridge lady fetched in Fred How's waggonette. Young Grace and cousin Gladys went along, and remember the horse setting off before Fred was aboard. Shouts of 'whoa' as he ran behind went unheeded, but a thoughtful Station Master noting the frightened females, closed the gates until Fred arrived, all in the cause of 'Jam and Jerusalem'!

We remember the 'Dunstable Dasher' and many other passenger trains. We also recall goods like thousands of cattle for local dealers Bunkers, and apart from traffic mentioned elsewhere, by far the L.N.E.R.'s biggest customers were the Totternhoe Lime Company with chalk, bound for the Portland Cement Company at Rugby. Ninety year old Jess Pipkin recalled the locomotives he drove between 1926 and 1946. Names like Peckett, Aveling and Porter, Avonside and Manning Wardle No 1995, 21 tons built in 1920. Jottings from his diary note dates of new fire bars, tubes, pistons, valves, brake shoes, and buffers, he helped to fit. Even then he was shunting 2 train loads of 60 trucks a day for which the railway charged four pence a ton. Eventually 4 tracks to the quarry, and space for 200 trucks, carried

Stanbridgeford Station. When Park Farm milk was late, George Impey galloped with it to Leighton Buzzard to catch the train there! Photograph courtesy of Geoff Willmott.

Jess Pipkin on the footplate, with Len Turvey (Nebbie) on the buffers.

Despite a pusher tractor, Wynn's Diamond T got wheel spin delivering this 54 (ton) RB excavator, driven from new by Tommy Tritton. Bill Bodsworth backs a D8 down and pulls the lot up into the quarry in 1959.

up to 1,000 tons 4 times a day. Small wonder this station regularly held the award for the most goods traffic for its size in the U.K. About 400 yards of ³/₄" rope pulled an empty truck up an incline, via the weight of the loaded one going down. For 10 years I collected unworn lengths of discarded ropes that kept me in winch cable!

Of the lime kilns, Bert Proctor remembered drawing lime from the kilns so hot it burned the barrow. Another job was for them to show up to fifty tourists around the caves, from whence local lime stone was hewn. Lamps and candles were used along the passages, which ran a long way, but not to Dunstable, as sometimes supposed.

Arthur Roberts conveyed factory girls to Dunstable in a three-horse brake that also transported our football team. He was involved in organising a Hunt Meet in the 1930s.

Royal Grooms and Horseboxes outside Rye House (now Mick Reilly's residence) accompanied the three Royal Princes - Edward, later Duke of Windsor, George, who became King George VI and Henry, Duke of Gloucester - who, according to a National press cutting, were staying at Mentmore Towers.

The first Bus Service was the Reliance to Leighton Buzzard, operated by Pope of Hockcliffe. Len and Horace Bright ran a couple of Reo buses to the Rule and Square Inn. The first double decker (open top) was a Karrier owned by George Salter, which just cleared Church Street bridge. It was the conductor's duty to run upstairs warning everyone to 'duck down' each time it passed under. Eaton Bray men crewed a National bus kept at the Chequers Inn. On cold mornings, we would walk down to help start it, and were expected to dismount and push it up Lancot Hill when slippery. In return, before bus stops, the driver would toot an absent regular, and the conductor might come to your door. In fact the bus once reversed 60 yards when passengers announced one young lady was not on board.

Bob Palmer recalled Costin's AEC Charabancs, fitted with lorry bodies in the winter. For a trip to Yarmouth he would take a spare mag. axle shaft, a set of bearings, that could be fitted via a plate on the crankcase, 5 gallons of oil and 10 of water. A piece of good bacon rind in an ailing bearing had got him home more than once, he claimed. (More of Costin later) Years ago one could stand on Totternhoe Knolls in springtime and behold a white sea of fruit blossom as far as the eye could scan. Apple, cherry, greengage and damson, used one time by the Navy for dyeing.

The humble plum grew under any circumstances, as proved by Mr. Powell, who planted a sapling upside down for a bet - and still it grew into a tree.

Bird scaring with clapper, or muzzle loader gun, commencing at 4 a.m., was a regular occupation.

Harry Scott bought tons of fruit. Whole orchards, as it hung on the trees. His son, Gaius, stock piled baskets and boxes at collection points for their supplier, H. & J. W. Aldridge of High Wycombe, whose fleet of vehicles were well known hereabouts.

Gaius recalls that on one occasion a consignment of $12\frac{1}{2}$ tons of plums, contained in 1000 boxes, value £500 (the controlled price being 10 shillings a box), was waiting to go by rail when the track was bombed. Dick Lacey came to the rescue, putting 7 tons on Aldridge's AEC Monarch, 3 tons on her trailer, and shared the other $2\frac{1}{2}$ tons with a small lorry, much

Mr. Aldridge Snr. with Commer No.3, about 1920. Here we have a lesson in roping an unsheeted load, look closely and see.

*Dick Lacey (right)
and members of the
Aldridge staff, with
a fruit-laden Dennis
in the 1950s.*

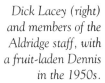

to the relief of the Scotts, and greatly preferable to worthless plum slurry. In those days 'Damson Wood' was no status address, but an orchard where part-time plum picking earned the rent.

It's hard to believe there was a time when hats were doffed as Squire Macnamara's coach drove along our High Street. When he ran up a big bill for horse shoeing Blacksmith George Brown's father stopped it out of the forge rent, only to be told "Stoppage is no substitute for payment, Brown". Small wonder when the Squire died someone remarked "Good job too". When word got back to the Manor this man was sent for, and made to apologise. Ted Brown recorded he had shod a horse for three shillings and repaired children's hoops for a penny. Many an unsuited horse was sold out of London. Jeff Archer said they became uncontrollable on seeing green fields beyond Edgeware. Riding bare back from London led to bleeding thighs and stiff buttocks.

My father tended poultry and reared many pigs. Jews from London would buy thousands of quality chickens. One, a Mrs Goldsmith, visited and paid cash, carried in the leg of her knickers. Grandpa had a livestock dealing 'rapport' with Harry Pool of Leighton Buzzard, despite the fact that one financed Methodism and the other the Brewers. My mother was impressed by the name Maurice which Mrs. Pool had given her son, and named the child she was carrying likewise. Maurice Pool emigrated to Australia for a time in 1924. Aged 17, he rode on a crate of live poultry to London, at the mercy of my grandpa, and the 'T' Ford. When the Standard Cable Company were laying telephone lines in 1925, two men cycled to Hockliffe, tossed a coin, for one job. Jess Pipkin (Park Lane) won, and travelled the country as far as Bristol and Leeds. The gang's bikes and gear would be stacked around the cable drums on one of E. W. Rudd's Scammells. Jess and his mate rode hundreds of miles, seated on the front wings of this vehicle. The telephone came to Eaton Bray in 1914, when Miller Bert Bunker applied, and was required to get a minimum of nine other subscribers. They were: The Post Office, No. 1, Bert Bunker, No. 2, A. Roberts, No. 3, The Vicar, No. 4, F Tooley, No. 5, A. Thorne, No. 6, W. Wallace, No. 7, C. Janes, No. 8, P. C. Hebbs, No. 9, J. Sanders, No. 10, who always shouted London calls, due to the distance involved! Linesman Bill Crees serviced cables from St. Albans to Bletchley on a bicycle.

Eaton Bray's first motorised wheels were the Rev. Sutton's 'Scout' car, and Mr Wallace's

In 1925, Jess Pipkin and his mate rode hundreds of miles seated on the front mudguards of this Scammell.

'Morse' MH4854, a touring car during World War One. Sid Copperwait opened the first garage and petrol pump, long before the Roebuck Garage, owned by Geoff James, now incorporating the old 'Bedford Arms Inn'. Sid's was the first taxi, a Studebaker, which he drove to Clacton and back the same day - an achievement for Sid, at least. Just up the road Loll Piggott opened a corrugated iron garage in 1927, on the site of the old Brickworks that ran from his father's cottage up to the rear of Booth Place. The many dell holes provided a rough circuit around which 10 year old Ron and younger Dennis Piggott would ride a World War One Douglas motor cycle. Later the garage was enlarged, and brick built for Ben Reeve, a fine lorry mechanic, who nursed Groves Latil over 40 years ago, and nurses mine to this day. 4 x 4 history was made here when David and Stuart Howe became the first civilian Jeep distributors in the U.K. in 1972. The first Jeep was sold to Contractor Charlie Nash of Leighton Buzzard. Pride of the showroom is a 1944 Willys Jeep originally used regularly by General Eisenhower in Scotland, and confirmed in writing.

Denis Sharrett ran a Jeep for 15 years from 1950. He still raves about its simplicity of maintenance, appetite for rugged use, and ability to stand being bulldozed 60 yards sideways by an artic.

This tenacious 4 x 4, built for the punishment of war, now often bought for prestige in peace, sired the Land Rover, and every known 4 x 4 in its class. The French family came to Park Farm in 1928. I relished the visits from Brooks of Mistley, near Colchester. The giant Armstrong Saurer, loaded with animal feed, would detach her trailer in the market place. I would be there, attempting to help hook up. The approaching drone of the vehicles like this, and that of Dunstable's Tilling Stevens Fire Engine coming to practise at the pond, drew me like a magnet. My greatest thrill was when grandpa visited the bank, and I waited outside, as great pioneers of transport, lorries like 'Rudd', 'Fisher Renwick', and 'Norman Box', would crawl up Dunstable's High Street (the A5) boiling and groaning south in low gear. Our various Constables nipped young offenders in the bud with a swing round the ear from their capes. One Eaton Bray youth, who felt unfairly accused of fatherhood after consorting with a young lady of easy virtue, put it to the Magistrate this way: "If you fell down in a bunch of nettles, could you prove which one had stung you, Sir"?

MILLS AND WINDMILLS

Two pairs of owls and dozens of pigeons surrendered their home for desirable residencies when Two Counties Mill, standing half in Bucks and Beds, was reduced to rubble in December 1988. "I saw it go up - I saw it come down" says eighty-five year old George Cook, referring to the massive water tank, insisted on by the insurers after the 1917 Mill fire. Gilberts, Engineers of Leighton Buzzard, had erected the tank, forging and riveting the sections in situ, some 68 feet high atop the tower.

Alfred Thorne, son of Charles the founder, was a milling baron of his day, and big provider of work, albeit hard, for this district. Four men would turn over the giant oil engine that drove the four-floored mill and generated power and lighting from the very latest storage battery system, whilst the rest of us struggled with paraffin lamps. Over twenty Mill Girls were employed just to pack Eclipse brand self-raising flour. A blind eye was turned to deprived children caught raiding the loads of stale biscuits direct from Lyons Corner House for grinding into pig meal.

You could leave school at thirteen if you had a job, and Stan Fountain was glad to work from 6.30 a.m. 'til 6 at night for eight shillings a week, as horse boy. 'Zulu' and 'Gipsy' were the spare team, but it was 'Sceptre' and 'Madam' his dad Ernest drove, with two tons in a double horse van. This trusted servant retailed direct to shops for miles around.

'Mann's' Patent Steam Cart and Waggon' Circa 1918 - read the plate affixed to a gleaming new steam lorry. George Cook and his pals stood gawping at this wonder of their time, when Alfred Thorne chided - "Well, you've had a good look, now clear off". This first iron wheeled steamer broke the river culvert under the road by the entrance and regularly cut deep ruts in the road all the way from Standbridgeford to the Mill, that generated as much controversy then as the demise of the Mill today. Probably because James A. Mann was a fellow sole proprietor, Alfred favoured his firm.

Excitement reigned in the Blake houshold. To quote: "Our dad, Abel, was to go up to a place called Leeds to collect the new steam lorry in 1920. A demonstrator seated at the second steering wheel, which enabled the mate to steer, whilst the drive stoked, brought 'Puffin Billy', as we called it, the long trip home at 12 m.p.h., then the speed limit." In fact, Stan Fountain, who became the regular mate, recalls a police trap one night on the A5. Abel was flashed by a lantern, and warned to 'watch it' since he had touched over $11^1/_2$ m.p.h.

Percy Blake, Abel's son, spent school holidays as tailboard boy. A typical day consisted of up to eighty calls out as far as Ware, Hertford, and Watford, always returning via Brown's Flour Mills, Luton for a back load. With a 6 a.m. fire up start, the working did not end till you got back. No tachometers in those days! A tankful of water from the 'Washbrook' (the one time sheep wash by Frank Peel's field), would take them twenty miles. Overloading and broken axles went hand in hand. Even so, Puffin Billy gave yeoman service.

Come 1925, the famous 'Mann Express' arrived, and proved her name by going to London twice, on many a long day. Built to carry six tons, nearer ten was the norm, and Bert Hazzard, Stan Warner, and Bob Jaggard made steam history hereabouts.

After World War One, Commer Cars of Luton were the victims of their own success, the market being saturated by secondhand ex W.D. vehicles. Alfred Thorne bought two ex army chain drive lorries. George Thorne (School Lane -no relation) landed the mate's job on the other without a windscreen. East winds on the Northampton run brought tears to his eyes.

Whole train loads of corn would come into Standbridgeford Station, where no driver dare pass empty. "Back carriage pays" Alfred would bellow regularly. At peak periods a load up from the station was expected before they commenced the day's work. Similarly, a jug of tea was found in the yard at night, calculated to replenish the strength to fetch another load from the busy goods yard.

It's the Ford Six Wheeler I remember most. During the war this remarkable vehicle creaked and groaned as she crossed over dozens of fire hoses in the London Blitz, loaded sky high twice daily, when conditions permitted. It was driven by little George Brinklow or big Bob Jaggard, who for a bet once carried a three hundred weight sack of cow cake up a flight of steps. All these men were humping 240lb sacks all day anyway. Alfred stayed with Fords, and later went on to V.8s and a 'Prefect' car, chauffeur-driven by young Carrie Lovell.

Uncle (as he was known) - Len Tearle - served in the office from 1921 until he retired from William Simmons of Leighton Buzzard. This company acquired Alfred Thorne, Eaton Bray Limited, in 1951. Others to transfer were Alfred's grandsons Roger and Richard, whose wife Mary was so helpful with photographs, yet sadly not spared to see the outcome. Few knew about Alfred's generosity, or just how much of his wealth was channelled into the Strict Baptist Chapel opposite. He gave the first Harmonium in 1902, and shared its playing with Ezra Janes, another stalwart family of this Bethel. The Janes have sold shoes since 1896. The great grandsons were not the first with 'the appliance of science'. Charlie Janes pioneered wireless accumulator charging hereabouts. Son Phil remembers packaging cycle lamp carbide. In 1936 the Duke of Windsor's abdication speech was broadcast in the National Schools from a box called a loudspeaker - the handiwork of electric man Charlie Janes. This man's other enterprise was the supply and servicing of Raleigh bicycles to transport men and women to Waterlow's Printing Works.

In 1844 Richard Simmons started in business at Bellows Mill, Eaton Bray. His son Frederick acquired a mill in Leighton Buzzard, and his son William, a bachelor, left the mill to two workers and nephews. One was Fred Tooley, who had the first Ford car in Eaton Bray. His son Peter bought Bellows Mill in 1960. Peter's widow, Vera, now Mrs. Wood, lives there today.

Edlesborough Windmill, a local landmark, lost its sails during a gale years ago, when someone omitted to lock them. In the nearby water mill, now beautifully restored by

144   Richard Grant, P.C. Tom Dennis, minus his helmet, sometimes joined a party of regulars who gathered for a session of sport. Perhaps twenty rats would be feeding on the stationary mill stone at night. An opened sluice would spin this like a turntable. Lanterns and sticks were the only aids required, plus the ability to hit the rats, and not your mates. The operation was repeated in an hour or so after refreshment for the participants!

'Sceptre' and 'Madam', the two smart grey horses Ernest Fountain drove to towns for miles around.

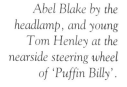

Abel Blake by the headlamp, and young Tom Henley at the nearside steering wheel of 'Puffin Billy'.

The famous 'Mann Express' – new in 1925, 9 to 10 tons was the norm for this 6-tonner. Two loads a day from London Docks (40 miles away) was achieved by men and a machine who seemed to know no limits of endurance.

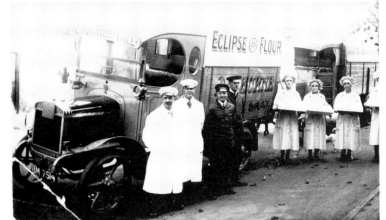

Two ex W.D. Commers, the older rear one had no windscreen. Drivers known from the left: Harry Bird, Bert Hazzard and Arthur Puddefoot.

'First Prize' says the card over the cab, when the mill girls adorned this Ford 6 wheeler for Watford Carnival, circa 1930s.

William Simmons steamers frequented Eaton Bray. Photograph courtesy of Austin James.

This Sentinel fascinated me when delivering pig feed to us.
Photograph courtesy of Mr. T. Lawson.

The Harper family – father and four sons drove this fleet of Dennis lorries.
My thanks to Austin Janes for all his help.

DUCKS

Years ago Eaton Bray was awash with ducks. Mr. Wallace started out with them. Arthur Holmes put carcasses, ordered by postcard onto a given bus, which would be met by a Luton Hotelier within the hour. Ducks were even driven loose to Standbridgeford station, and despatched live by rail. But by far our largest breeders were Maud and Ezra Tompkins in Moor End. Row upon row of orange boxes nested broody hens sitting on twelve eggs for twenty-eight days throughout the spring months to produce an average of two to three thousand ducks a year. Son Clifford knows the real meaning of the saying - 'Like a dying duck in a thunderstorm'! At the slightest sign of heavy rain, baby ducks in pens of fifty would have to be driven under cover or they would stand, beak open skyward, and virtually drown. Plucking commenced at 5 a.m. daily. By 8 a.m. sharp, wicker baskets were loaded onto a horse-drawn cart destined for Standbridgeford and the ducks were in Leadenhall Market, London, by midday. Eight acres of fruit trees were Ezra's other source of income. Buyers from London, Leicester, and even Manchester, vied for his plums. Clifford's memories of four or five visits a day to the Post Office, to telegraph prices, demonstrates this old man's shrewd dealing. In one night, the family weighed up and packed two tons in twenty four pound baskets, lined with a wisp of hay, covered in newspaper, secured by two crossed-over willow laths, all by the light of a cycle gas lamp.

Pigs were to be Clifford's main line, and wartime recollections include such supplementary rations as 'Tottenham Pudding', the name given to waste restaurant food so direct from the table that it always contained a few cups, saucers, cutlery and ashtrays.

Accepted as a brilliant amateur photographer from the 1930s, this man's home is filled with magnificent works of his art.

For over two years now he has fought the dreaded skin complaint, psoriasis, which took him to the depths of despair, but thanks to Dr. Twivey and wife Nancy, he is winning through.

Thousands of ducks were bred in Eaton Bray, young Clifford Tompkins snapped these in 1925.

CARNATIONS

"Mr. Wallace might claim to be the best carnation grower in the world, and not be challenged", reads an article in a Nursery Journal circa 1924. Mr. & Mrs. W. E. Wallace came to Eaton Bray, starting a general nursery in 1886. The sea of water-like eight and a quarter acres of glass seen from the Chilterns grew from four glazed-over duck houses, and closed in 1974. From 1904 success in the perpetual flowering carnation was to put, and keep, W. E. Wallace a leading name in the trade. Sid, Max, and Bernard Sharrett built a new greenhouse every two years, each either 200 or 250 feet long by 45 feet wide. The last one, a 300 footer, is still used by Paul Bashford to this day. These structures were in pitch pine, sheer engineering in wood. Basil Ruffett recalls the water tower housed three giant Ruston engines 'clonking away' to deliver 80,000 gallons of water daily from three 300 feet artesian wells. 450,000 continuous growing plants had quite a summer thirst in temperatures that could reach 100 degrees, a test of endurance for many of the 100 employees. In winter 50 tons of best anthracite a week was consumed. On becoming oil fired, Bulkwark Transport tankers delivered 3,000 gallons of oil three times a week. I was on hand with my winch when one of these loads slipped into the brook. However, A5 Garage got the recovery call with their 'Diamond T'. Only after the professionals gave up on the job did Mr. Robins of Wallace's ask if I would have a go. A little crowd gathered as 'Eunice' raised her bonnet to the heavens, extracting the artic for less money than A5's call-out charge.

I remember the boast that W. E. Wallace Carnations featured at Royal Garden Parties, via Court Florists. Favourite varieties like "Delight", "Margaret Kay", "Enid" and "Royalty" are to live on as names on the Wallace Drive estate.

The Wallace 500 acre farm and fruit trees were a separate entity. A gifted gardener, Joe Baker, who carried the Salvation Army Flag, grafted thousands of the apple stock that produced vast crops. Mr. Wallace's son-in-law, Ernest Gray, questioned the economics of Eddie Impey galloping along the Baulk on a pony just to 'trace horse' draw Will Henley's horse and trolley up Lancot Hill with 40 bushels of apples. Therefore in 1925 a new Morris Commercial lorry was bought. Sid Bearton was given five shillings to get a licence. Two trips to St. Albans with John Sear, and he became the first driver. In a good year, 10,000 dozen blooms a day were despatched all over the U.K. Each month Sid would take a £1,000 cheque for rail charge to Standbridgeford. During the war, 500 tons of tomatoes one summer made another record.

Mr. and Mrs. Wallace and daughters Hattie and May were held in the highest esteem locally. Little is known of their great generosity, save the benefactors themselves, and they would never have had it otherwise.

One of the three Ruston engines in the water tower.

Wallace's favoured Morris Commercials. TM 5907 was the first. Sid Bearton, Harry Ashwell and Johnny Bartle line up for this snapshot.

Load after load of well roped boxes of carnations went all over the UK. Note the folding step and cab top standing platform as always specified.

The packing shed. Charlie Tibbett and driver Ted Willis. Photographs courtesy of Ted Willis.

SHARRETTS

A big Clydesdale horse kicked Matt Hazzard so hard he spun like a top across the Moor End yard, landed badly, and became mentally deranged. Two men with a dog cart got as far as Aylesbury, bound for Stone Asylum with Matt, when the horse slipped over on ice. Quite unable to raise the horse, the men unfettered this giant blacksmith, who single handed lifted the horse, thus unknowingly ensuring his journey into incarceration for life. Such was the life and time of Sharretts, Master Builders, Undertakers, and Farmers of Eaton Bray.

Space permits but a glimpse of this exceptional family. Sarah and Jeffrey Sharrett, Carpenter by trade, had eleven children - six girls and five boys, an appetite for hard work, and an acumen for business. Within a few years, Saturdays would see some thirty building and farm workers jostling for each trade's right to be paid first. Each Sunday plans were made for both departments around a big table, also at Yew Tree Farm.

Sharretts felled, hauled, and sawed much of their own timber. Seventy trees alone from the park one year. Two Sawyers walked from Leighton Buzzard and worked the pit saw, sixty four hours a week. They would chant "We're by the day" as they slowly sawed. Once a price was fixed they speeded up, changing the chant to "We've got the job". Sons Sid and Max walked miles, even to Studham, to work. Records show the bosses' sons were paid 17s.6d. per 50 hour week in 1895. Sharrett craftsmanship lives on in St. Mary's Church. The doors, chancel screen and magnificent organ loft stairway (no longer there) are all works of art. The rebuilt tower and roof cross members weighing almost a ton, were hewn and raised by Sharrett-designed derrick, powered by Jeffrey's horse team, a great achievement in 1922!

Sid's son, Bernard, bared his soul to me, in the 1800's workshop that remained, like him, little changed in 1985. Later Sid had owned a car. A tiller steered three-wheeled 'A.C.' it seems. "I used to dread folk dying in these epidemics; years ago half of Summerleys was wiped out you know. I was only sixteen when I measured my first corpse, an old 'gel' who had died in Leighton hospital, so I didn't hang about". It seems Bernard stopped his motor bike at Slapton, reflected on the hasty measurement, and added a few inches to be on the safe side. He continued - "After the funeral, our Dad said: I say, boy, let's see your rule, it's different to mine! I bet you guessed the size, being 'frit' to catch the fever".

Sharrett accountancy was simple, each Client's hours and materials were pencilled on a board off-cut. When full, these were taken over to 'Yew Tree', entered into a ledger, then the board was planed clean and used again.

'Vallance End Farm' is poorish ground. Eldest son Thomas tended this and 'Yew Tree', where his brother George, gassed in World War One, and his sisters 'slaved' rather than worked to keep going.

Tom's second son, Denis, the last of this amazing family, still farms Vallance End, where Tom brought Eaton Bray's first tractor, a Ford model 'F', secondhand in 1925. When it broke down, one of the farm's eight horses, a black mare, with Herculean strength, pulled this wormdriven tractor home. Up to 500 sheep kept Dunstable Downs free of scrub from the London Gliding Club, stretching from Wellhead to Bison Hill, previously Sharrett owned. Incidentally, the first car ever to ascend Zoo Hill was a model 'T' Ford. The coming of the Zoo in 1931 brought early thunderstorm warnings, heralded by roaring Lions, who still sense bad storms. Peacocks flew over the fence and fed with the hens. Their beauty was not valued by the foxes, or the local man who said 'they ate like turkeys'. An escaped grizzly bear apprehended a motor cyclist, who ran off. This powerful animal picked up the motor bike, and threw it over the hedge after him.

Tom had a hollow rib cage where a waggon had run over him. I remember seeing him approach the Plough crossroads, applying his cycle brakes, the soles of his feet on the ground. But he'd misjudged an oncoming car's speed. It hit him, and stopped as he rolled off the bonnet. The ambulance men mistakenly attended the motorist, who had fainted. Tom, badly lacerated, was up the road looking for his pump. No way would he go to hospital! Falling from a loft one Christmas, a rusty spike tore open his scalp so badly his face actually dropped. When it was sown up his head resembled a laced up football. Even so this tough old man lived on to his 91st year.

Scrawled on a stable wall to this day are the words 'Albert Simmons -Standard II - the total schooling of a deaf and dumb boy, whose entire working life was made possible because Tom and the family wrestled for hours teaching him a farm sign language they devised that enabled this unemployable lad, who walked daily from Taskers row, to become a most gifted horseman. The Sharretts tended to refuse to progress in some ways, yet they were a family of ideas and great workaholics. In employer attitudes to the handicapped, Thomas Sharrett was fifty years before his time.

These ploughing engines were working for Jeffrey Sharrett down The Rye during W.W.1.

Jeffrey Sharrett (left) by the steam plough.

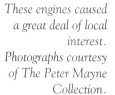

These engines caused a great deal of local interest. Photographs courtesy of The Peter Mayne Collection.

Eaton Bray's first tractor! Sid Weedon ploughing opposite Vallance End Farm in 1926. The radiator casting suggests this model 'F' Ford was new about 1917.

Tom Sharrett cutting corn in 1928. This snapshot won a prize in a competition.

Harvest cart in the 1930s, as the Zoo Lion was being made. One wet year they were still harvesting on Armistice Day (November 11th). At 11a.m. George Sharrett ordered Cliff Tompkins "Stop the horse and take your cap off" – such was the respect then. Photograph courtesy of Clifford Tompkins.

PIONEERING LUTON'S MOTORS

I can just remember a burly overalled mechanic on a motor bike. Why did he jack up a rear wheel, engage top gear, and swing the starting handle? (a practice that could kill, if a poorly jacked vehicle started up and toppled). He was checking the magnet gaps on the flywheel of Grandad's model 'T' Ford lorry it seems. I chatted as Bill Liberty served petrol at the garage he has run for 54 years, at the corner of Boscombe Road, Dunstable.

This 82 year old man's life in motoring started around 1927 with The Luton Motor Company Ltd, sole Ford Agents, established in 1919, jointly with Motor Bodies, who did the coachwork. Another veteran of those days, still going strong, is Oliver Bradshaw at his garage in Westoning. Perhaps twice a week these lads would catch the 5.19 a.m. train bound for Trafford Park, Manchester, bringing back cabless solid tyred chassis on a horsehair seat in all weathers, avoiding holes in the road, and tramps who would try to climb aboard. It took two days, and is far removed from today's 'trade plate boys'. The 'T' Ford was so simple, a mechanic could easily fit a crown wheel wrong way round, thus giving one forward and two reverse gears as one was to find starting up, looking backward, and running forward into a wall.

Ford tractors (before the registered company of Ford and Son ('Fordson') were off-loaded at Luton station. These were far too stiff to crank by the handle, and were started via a long special 'L' shaped lever. These early tractors had fierce clutches that had just two

82 year old Bill Liberty still running his garage forecourt in 1989 – open for service from 6 in the morning.

One of 'Motor Bodies' Luton vans in London, circa 1920. I can remember Luton thronging with lorries like this.

positions 'in or out'. I also traced Len Allen, who was thirty-six years with Motor Bodies. He remembered Thorne's Fords, and building many of the famous 'Luton Bodies'. The additional 5ft long x 6ft wide 3ft high space built over the cab was nicknamed the 'Bedroom' he tells me.

Dave Tompkins was our first Auto Electrician; trained at Luton Motor Company, he set up a unique mobile repair unit.

Bertram Edgar Barrett was just five feet two inches high; in every other respect this little man was a giant. Being motor mad, and a Methodist, overrode my lack of education, and B.E.B. as he was known, accepted me aged fourteen in April, 1937, as an apprentice motor engineer. The five shilling weekly bus ticket halved my wage, which rose to one pound in the fourth year.

Thirteen year old Bertie Barrett, himself apprenticed as a general engineer, gained a certificate in motor engineering at night school, such were the abounding energies of the young man who opened Luton's first garage in Langley Street, around 1910. Four years later a prominent Estate Agent and relative Benjamin Franklin became imbued with the lad's predictions of motor transport. The vast garage in Castle Street, that runs through from Union to Holly Street, little changed and owned by Kennings today, was a blending of these two men's faith and finance.

A brilliant career as a violinist awaited Olive Barrett, but she opted for her sweetheart's dream, and working with him. Bertie would start at 7 a.m. and often could still be found in the workshop at ten o'clock at night. The Barrett progress is best traced in the 'Luton News' archives. He held the Ford agency in 1918 prior to the Luton Motor Company. 'Heated well lit garage for 200 cars' - 'Sole Humber Agency' - 'Agent for Palladium Heavy Lorries' - 'Biggest Garage in the County' - his adverts were prolific. By now three charabancs named with B.E.B. in mind were called 'Busy Bee', 'Buzz Buzz' and 'Buoyant Breezer' - for seaside trips and hire. During the Motor Show this enterprising man ran a charabanc shuttle to Olympia, to conduct prospective clients round the stands.

Up to ten lorries by Palladium, Selden, AEC and Daimler formed a versatile haulage fleet, managed by one William Parrott, a man of ideas. The first of these was evening mystery tours with the charas., very popular with car-less Lutonians.

Now these heavy lorries transporting Luton-made hats to London already had long and the highest possible bodies of fixed tarpaulin, supported by ash hoops. How to increase the capacity without a trailer came to Bertie one day, chatting with Bill Parrott - the two men's imagination ran riot! Why not bring the body out over the cab and support it with two iron stays beside the radiator? This would add 90 cubic feet capacity for hats. That day the idea of the 'Luton Van' was conceived by two Luton men. In no time Motor Bodies Ltd were building the 'Barrett Parrott dream' for everyone - it was never patented. Bill Parrott had other dreams of hauling heavier goods than hats. The steam lorry was waiting for him to exploit, and he moved on. Another notable young man, Harold Wilson, came in 1929, worked in, later managed and became a director of the haulage side until the fleet was sold to Stephens Removals in 1979, and he went with it. By 1936 the solid tyred heavies had all gone, save one Daimler, which had a crude but efficient rear gantry that served as a day and night recovery vehicle throughout World War Two. The fleet then consisted of four Bedford Luton Vans (one six wheeler) on daily London service. A fast Surrey Dodge did Birmingham three times a week. Two small Ford vans collected boxes of finished hats from the 300 plus Hat Factories in the town, and these were sorted and loaded overnight ready for delivery next day, each load consisting of about 500 boxes. My greatest affection was for 'The Old Grey Lady' a 1931 Ford six wheeler, finished in battleship grey, and never painted B.E.B. green. This was the first lorry I every drove unofficially. She was never the same after sand bag carting in 1939, which was a bit much for the 'O.G.L.' as I recall. During the war Harold Wilson was required to drive a Ministry van by day and operate the haulage by evening and night. War work included collecting various suppliers' parts for Vauxhall Motors, and when the Luton Hat Trade declined rapidly in the 70s, a big contract was secured for six lorries to deliver spares daily to Vauxhall dealers in a radius of over fifty miles, one for every year Harold had served Barretts.

The old A6 runs into Castle Street from Harpenden, as did business residents who chose to garage their prestigious autos where 24 hour service was via the new 'Theo' petrol pump that selected and served eight brands. By the office was a bell button, 'Ring for Service'. The moment it rang, you ran, not walked. "Service is what has put me, and will keep me, ahead of others" B.E.B. insisted. I was given a chamois leather solely to clean the rear windows and windscreens of up to a hundred cars parked in any one day. No one must leave with a dirty windscreen. Impatient clients would drive through the garage with me performing from the running board, leaping off at the door, to B.E.B.'s delight. I was responsible to three garage hands, three mechanics, and a foreman. My first job was to help a mechanic (who hated Fords) to fit a transverse spring. Battered, bruised, and bleeding, he adopted a stance of prayer, closed his eyes and repeated a skit on the 23rd Psalm - "The Ford is my car, I'll never have another, it maketh me to lie down in damp places, and anointeth my head with oil; my sump runneth over. Surely our Lizzie should run on R.O.P. at a shilling a gallon, but it won't. Now the Austin will, for ever and ever, amen". (My repetition of this recitation did not amuse my mother, who reminded me of sacrifices made for me to learn worthwhile knowledge.)

The spacious top end of the garage housed the lorries, and up to twenty new chassis on delivery nightly. Bedford, Commer, and W.D. Karrier were parked in order of collection times.

I would partially inflate an inner tube that was to be the cushion. A bit of sheeting stuck under the bonnet, and tied back to the wooden seat offered little protection in winter, en route to Spurlings in London, Gatley Autos in Manchester, or even Scotland. Another duty was to clean and oil the wheels of a hydraulic trolley jack. During dinner hour I would test this with the 'T' handle locked vertically. I would push hard, leap aboard, and glide at speed down the garage, like a child on a scooter. One day I slipped off, and the jack careered on, fortuitously passing Mr. Dandy's Rolls, Hubbard Ltd's Lagonda and the big Talbot belonging to Sir Frederick Mander. My luck ran out when a new Austin Goodwood stopped it, and I wept as I examined the buckled doors and shattered glass. In the office a torrent of words from B.E.B., starting with "You barmy josser" ended in "You will be sent home for three days", as he towered over me, verbally, at least. Mother was even more displeased.

As customers left their cars they would request me to mend a puncture, check tyres, battery, water, oil, or say "fill her up" - famous last words of a Mr Aspinall one busy day. Next morning in the office an irate Mr. A. relived running out of petrol halfway home in a thunderstorm and my further negligence cost me another three days. Prior to this, I was working on my half days on a 'written off' twelve year old Austin 7 tourer I had bought for three pounds. I had applied for my driving test on becoming seventeen, which came up a week after the Aspinall fracas. Unpainted, and almost roadworthy, my steed reluctantly came to a stop at the test office. I was underneath still adjusting the brakes when the examiner appeared. To my horror it was none other than the portly Mr. Aspinall, who flopped into the temporary passenger seat, which collapsed and left him looking toward the heavens throughout the test. In panic I flooded the engine as I cranked it up which led to a hasty plug change. Despite this, I was called 'Mr.' and treated as a perfect stranger, even as I extricated this Gentleman, who was by then congratulating me at the end of the test on passing. We often talked later, but our professional meeting was never mentioned.

Another B.E.B. innovation was the only solid tyre press for miles around, rescued, and still used, by Barry Weatherhead of Woburn Sands. Mention must be made of Mr. Barrett's pride and joy Daimler, 'The Chariot'. He had discovered it rotting away in a field. Making mostly new parts it was lovingly restored and used as a fund raiser, both for the Hospital and his Methodist Church in Chapel Street, Luton. This brilliant man was a human 'Crypton Tester', who could diagnose most engine faults by listening to the exhaust outlet, and gave me hours of tuition in his workshop. A perk of the job was to get to test drive some very fine cars. Having helped service a Railton straight eight, foreman Sam Temple was soon hurtling us down the old A6. What a thrill at that time to get up to 85 m.p.h. and still have power to spare. Yet few of my friends could believe me.

Ever planning for the future, B.E.B.'s son, Roy, was at this time working for Perkins Engines of Peterborough. The late Frank Perkins had driven a 'Wolf' engined Hillman car to Russia on a promotional exercise. About this time Roy took a similar car around New Zealand. This further story of Barrett enterprise will never be told, since sadly Roy has now passed away. However, I am most indebted to his widow, Margaret, for the loan of some fine photographs, and for long talks with Mr. Barrett's daughter, Dora. Sculpture has been her life's work, and she is surrounded by metal and wood brought to life by her hands. By far her greatest challenge came in a commission to design and create in bronze a work that embodied a Queen and Cross. Today this work of art stands in Queen Eleanor's Shopping Precinct in Dunstable. Therefore, although there are no Barrett children, the name will live on hereabouts.

The remarkable man who made motoring milestones in Luton continued to drive until he was eighty-five, and lived to be ninety-one. I last saw him when I did tree work at his home. As I left, he wiped my driving mirror and commanded "Give 'em good service you know"!

The Barratt Garage that ran from Union Street through to Holly Street. I swept this floor from door to door many a time.

One of the three charabancs at Luton Hoo gate.

A prestigious car and customer.

The 1899 Daimler 'The Chariot' in 1935. Bertie loved to use this for charity work.

Mr. Barrett and son Roy make a retirement presentation to mechanic Cecil Sexton.

MORE PIONEERS

William Thomas Parrott was paraffin man at Caddington. An early contract was to carry canned petrol across the fields to Vauxhall Motors when they came to Luton. He went on to establish the Town's first fleet of heavy transport, and was a popular Methodist local preacher.

After two other venues, the imposing building at the top of Kingsway, Luton, was home to his two companies, W. T. Parrott Transport and West Park Engineering. These companies were 'Gardner' accredited Sales and Service dealers, and area Agents for 'Foden'. This enterprising man diversified from buses and charabancs to the haulage of heavy goods, sand and hats. New vehicle sales ranged from a Peugeot 5 cwt Van (£135 in 1929) to Foden eight wheelers. He was assisted by his two sons, Frank and Rex. Rex was a former Barrett apprentice, who was held up as an example to me whenever he called back at the garage with his gleaming black Alvis car. Steamers gave way to 'Foden' diesels, Luton's first in fact, and members of the 'Foden' family often visited and stayed with Rex.

After the nationalisation of Road Transport, Parrott brothers Colin and Norman, Rex's sons, concentrated on the engineering side, and do so to this day. True, they vacated the top building in 1988, and gave up trying to sell petrol from a host of former petrol pumps in Luton's busy Dunstable Road, but business is as usual down the ramp. In the lower building, where temperatures would remain degrees higher on a winter's night as the fleet of 'Fodens' with their hot engine, gearbox, and axle oils acted as a unique mass night storage heater. The Parrott tradition lives on.

The names of 'Foden' and 'Gardner' made transport history in Luton, which is not bad going for a humble oil man, and local preacher.

The Parrott Brothers recalled the pride of one of their drivers - Spencer Smith. Polished brass autovac pipes were part of his immaculately turned out vehicles. My meeting with this 83 year old was not by his fireside but over the desk of his son Martin's van business, between telephone calls and puffs at his pipe.

Spencer's amazing life in steam and diesel unfolded with fascination. At about twenty years old he started with Thurstons, the Showmen of Norwich, according to a faded reference.

He took over the showman's engine 'Alexandra' from new, but it was the Burrell scenic showman's engine 'Victory' which was his favourite. No words of mine can describe his taking her from Rushden to Hull with three long trailers and water cart, grossing at about seventy tons. "You had to watch the corners you know" he said, with a wink. That was his summer job. Each winter was spent in Scotland, driving a shunting locomotive pulling sugar beet.

His first waggon at Parrotts in 1936 was a Foden No. 22 and trailer. He covered thousands of miles with a rare 'Chinese6' with 12 ton up. She was a 'proper heavy on the handlebars' he stressed. The love of his life was MJ 625 ERF's very first 8 wheeler new to W. T. Parrott. Eventually, Spencer took her over after an entire rebuild. Only the wheels and gearbox were original; and a new longer chassis gave her a 24 foot bed. "What a waggon! I was on the Scotland run in those days. Do you know Brauston Hill that long drag from Willoughby? She would come up there many a time with 14 ton on in third. Not too many were doing that then."

Later Spencer was to do sixteen years with nearby Laporte Chemicals. Running to Purfleet and Redhill with 14 tons 6 cwt of sulphuric acid up behind him with a single drive 8 wheeled AEC tanker, which could be a 'real cow' on ice when empty. Did acid-carrying all those years worry him? "I've romped round Shepherds Bush with a few thousand gallons; it can be nasty stuff to handle!"

Come the war, every haulier came under the Ministry of War Transport. Loads and allocations ceased to be contracts but became orders, 'tall ones' most of them, and drivers took them without question. Journeys operated at 'suicide rates', often in suicide conditions, through bombs and fires, with side lights reduced to the diameter of a ten pence piece, often along damaged roads as the enemy sought to destroy our supply lines. Fuel and tyres were rationed, with ninety per cent of rubber production in occupied countries. The civilian driver was locked in his or her own war.

Spencer and the ERF hauled canned petrol, bombs, ammunition and gun mats. A lot more destruction would have been caused, in addition to the tragic loss of 23,000 houses destroyed by the V.1. Pilotless plane - The Flying Bomb - had not the command come to rush all the big guns out of London down to the coast. Suddenly, every 6 and 8 wheeler available was directed to transport gun mats, 12 x 12 timber baulks bolted to railway line lengths for gun bases. The ERF was one of six other Parrott vehicles working round the clock on this with other firms. Spencer was queuing to load in Harlow, and running to Rye in Sussex. A despatch rider would meet him in Sevenoaks, and take him right on to the beach, where soldiers unloaded by hand, shoving the ERF off when required. 'Red eyed' he would return in the blackout, time after time.

Of road transport, Winston Churchill said - "This is a war of unknown warriors". Spencer Smith and his kind were among their number.

Bill Parrott takes on a load of 2 gallon petrol cans at the LNER goods yard in Crescent Road. Peter Maynes father tells me the horses were required to stand on sleepers, obviating a spark risk from the horseshoes.

West Park Garage by day.

West Park Garage by night.

A six wheeled Sentinel steam lorry, new and on trade plates.

A fine example of the 'Luton Body' – the Parrott-Barrett invention that revolutionised hat transport.

Rex Parrott with 'The Beech Hill Safety Coach'. Another Parrott diversification.

One of the first Foden diesel lorries.

Solid tyre recovery, with trailer on board.

No.28 comes to grief and Fodens send out a test vehicle to tranship the load.

Spencer Smith did thousands of miles with this Foden, remarking "With 12 ton up she was proper heavy on the handlebars".

This shot was taken because Spencer's ERF was the only clean lorry in a row of six. Once, in Scotland, he was ordered a return load of sheepskins and refused due to possible damage to the paintwork. It was Friday, wartime, and no other load was available, but he was adamant, stayinmg over in the cab until Monday. Such was his pride. Spencer kept his HGV licence until he was 80!

FROM STEAM TO DIESEL

Edwin Richard Foden (ERF to you) foresaw the demise of steam, and left the family firm in 1932 to realise his diesel dream. Much midnight oil was burned at Hilary House in Elworth, as he, son Dennis, and former colleagues Ernest Sherratt and George Faulkner, designed their first lorry in the conservatory. In spite of the secrecy surrounding it, Rex Parrott 'got wind' of the project. When his cousin Fred Gilbert of Leighton Buzzard considered a rival make, he was urged to wait for the lorry Rex had predicted would be a sensation. Rex was right, and so was Edwin, and the rest is history. MJ 2711 was driven out of its birthplace shed by Madge, Edwin's wife, who had done the paperwork, mopped up the blood, sweat, and tears of the confinement of the first ERF, and later demonstrated how a woman can drive a 7 tonner. Brian Gilbert, then aged 12, has vivid memories of September 1933, and the lorry that had no fan or self-starter - a vehicle that was to do 250,000 miles carting Leighton Buzzard tiles for the next 20 years. The lorry worked 7 days for ages, since each weekend Edwin Foden loaned it for demonstration. This ensured Fred Gilbert free service and a free biannual overhaul, and a full order book at Sun Works. This was the first ERF that Marston Valley Bricks, and many other firms ever saw, tried, and bought from. The lorry's first journey was to Southend, and this became a regular run. My old friend, Eddie Pool (Van Hire), rode miles in her as mate. Later Brian took over the 8 ton loads of tiles, as well as three other vehicles, all ERFs of course.

The first ERF, MJ 2711,
and the men that made it.
From left to right:
Sam Gregory (test driver),
Jack Faulkner (fitter),
George Faulkner (works manager),
Danny Davenport (fitter),
and Wilf Kirk (electrician).
Later sold after 250,000 miles
with Fred Gilbert.

Bill Quantrill with his first ERF.

Bill Quantrill relished taking over this new 8 wheeler in 1937. It brought his money up to £3.15s. a week. The name Vandyke was changed to Stonehenge because of the Dutch implications.

Ironically, when I visited 96 Bassett Road, a current model raced past, the driver little knowing that for ERF, of course, this was hallowed ground. Bill Quantrill's ERF coming up the village at 4 a.m. was so punctual that my father timed his sleepless hours by him, in the 1960s and 70s. Bill, when aged only 18, was driving a six wheeled Garrett steamer. Previously he had been the mate, and bogged down on a building site, his driver had ordered "fire her up 'till she's blowing off, I'm going for some fags". On return, he jammed a hammer between the safety valve and cab roof and with a sudden burst of power out she came from the mud.

Quantrill Transport included brothers Les and Ron, all pro ERF. The Company Q.M.T. Vehicle Services, is run by the sons today.

A lesser known fact is that within 3 days of the first ERF being sold at one end of the town, Ted Foden landed another order with H. G. Brown & Sons in Stanbridge Road, Leighton Buzzard. A 5 L.W. was specified for this, the first of 5 to come. Later an order of 10 lorries for Stonehenge Brickworks, Leighton Buzzard, gave ERF a good start. Ted Foden became a friend of the Brown family and taught grandson, Pentus, (so named, being the fifth child) to skate in 1933. In 1949 Ted drove the first 'DG' Foden down on demonstration. The ERFs ended an era of steam for Browns, then running 5 Sentinel 'DG 6s' with stocks of 250 tons of coal a time to fire them. Previously a fleet of ex World War One Pierce Arrow lorries were their first vehicles.

Leighton Buzzard stands on sand, and the ERFs with trailers were delivering 15 tons of sand a time into London for $37^1/2$ pence worth of diesel. One ran for 17 years. When a rear axle was required, Pentus drove grandfather Harry up to Sandbach in his Buick car. "Don't send it, we'll take it" said H.B. Duly ERF staff manhandled the big Kirkstall axle crossways between the two rear Buick doors, which were tied half open to the hubs. This, and grandfather weighing 32 stone (yet he lived to be 90) had some bearing on a tyre burst near home, but they limped to the yard without a tyre on the wheel!

The Brown fleet lines up in Pages Park prior to nationalisation in 1949. Pentus in trilby hat, with young John, is beside the fifth lorry from the left. Pentus undertook to manage the local British Road Services depot, which he stuck for a week! Later he had the satisfaction of buying the depot and some of his previous vehicles.

It is not surprising Pentus had the first two Foden two-stroke engined waggons he could get. These fantastic vehicles turned a few heads as they roared up Lake Street on bulk cement haulage to Dereham, Norfolk, twice a day, when required. Today it's the 'norm'. Over 30 years ago, it was a record. I remember 'Toby' the Bulldog who, when ordered, tugged a rope to toll a ship's bell by the office to summon Pentus from up the yard. Later there were other 'Bulldogs' on the fronts of the fleet of Macks that great-grandson John ran across Europe. Soldiers in World War One nicknamed Macks 'The Bulldog' and it stuck.

I still recall an early ERF that brought ballast to the Lodge. Its number was written in my numberplate book. Hence the Brown memories in this one.

Derrick Bonfield and his sister, Joan, searched fruitlessly for the photograph of their father's old Leyland, which was to be Eaton Bray's first motor lorry and haulage contractor. When a half shaft failed in Rotherhithe tunnel Alf Bonfield and 9-year-old Derrick boarded a tram with the hefty parts, bound for spares at the Elephant and Castle. That night he fitted the new shaft, and a policeman lifted the sleeping child from the cab and carried him to the comfort of a stove in a nearby garage. I remember Alf collecting Derrick from school to help load lime at Totternhoe, bound for Oxfordshire. This was no joyride. All Sharrett's building materials were delivered on site. When Powdrills built High Town, Luton, Derrick became adept at the perilous art of 'block boy' as the Leyland 'jumped' Ampthill Hill with 7 tons of bricks, twice daily. His mother shed a tear as the Leyland left, being replaced by the gleaming new Bedford ticking over outside Shepherds Cottage on Tring Road, Eaton Bray. When the meagre petrol supply for the delivery by Shaw and Kilburn ran out, Derrick recalls that 2 gallons of petrol was a ton weight for a little lad to fetch 3 miles on foot from Downs Garage.

Derrick was just 16 years old when father became chronically ill, and the family business was in jeopardy. Alf had no choice, "Take my lorry, and my licence, until you get your own next year". Bonnie, as some call him, became a lorry driver overnight. His biggest problem was not getting the loads into London, but the consignees who required to deal 'with the driver', not the mate!

We next met whilst timbering in Bucks in the 1950s. Derrick had his uncle's 6 x 4 Morris Commercial chained to one tree, as he pulled another. The tree went sideways. Some of the Morris went backwards, but at least the front part remained, chained in position!! His daily deadline was to collect the 'fellers' by 5 p.m. after a load of pitprops up to Nuneaton. Yet another Bedford was driven to its limits. I came into transport from sheer enthusiasm, Derrick came from sheer necessity.

This snapshot of Derrick Bonfield with haulage contractor Ken Browning's Leyland twin steer was taken in 1959. Derrick was running twice a day to Dagenham with 14 tons of sand, shovelling every grain off by hand.

JOE AND ARTHUR -
BOB AND EDWIN

CAPITALISM AND CHRISTIANITY

"It is easier for a camel to go through the eye of a needle than for a rich man to enter into the kingdom of God." - Jesus Christ.

Anne Miller listened intently in Reigate Methodist Sunday School, her Superintendent, Arthur Rank, was reading from 'The Robe'. He had bought it in the U.S.A. prior to publication here. Lord Rank (as he became), like his famous father Joseph, was a non-smoking, non-drinking Methodist miller and Sunday School Teacher extraordinaire.

Years before, young Joe Rank lay asleep on a sack of bran in his father's Windmill in Hull. When the customer called for it father said 'Tak' the lad as well as the bran, he's good for nowt - he'll never be much use in the world!' From that slumbering body emerged a dynamic brain that was to replace the vagaries of the wind with the first triple-expansion 500 h.p. engine to go into a flour mill. Noise protests were met with - "It only runs from 6 a.m. until 10 p.m. and never on Sundays". Joseph introduced profit sharing, as a few shillings were set aside for workers. Little wonder they stayed long with him. 'J.R.' came from Primitive Methodist stock, 'The Ranters', who raved about their beliefs, rather than serve in silence.

Almost fearful of his abilities to create wealth he heeded the precepts of John Wesley "We will live on half or less of our income" he declared to his wife. Sifting the cadgers from the needy was a prosperity problem he'd discussed with God. Joseph gave thousands of pounds to hospitals and the poor of his native Hull. Every branch of Methodism benefited from his millions, quite apart from his £300,000 Benevolent Fund. This multi-millionaire's life style was the essence of frugality. In fifty years he never missed Sunday School, except for holidays, or business abroad. Whilst fellow captains of industry played golf, J.R. would visit and teach his beloved children. Moving to London, he reported to the nearest Sunday School, where there were no teacher vacancies. "What about your disruptive children? Let me take them", he challenged. The result was astonishing. Seeking a less ornate church for his Silvertown workers, he found most of the £33,000 to build Tooting Methodist Mission (based on three similar halls he built in Hull) and filled the 1,700 seats regularly. This giant of the international wheat markets retained the common touch. Asked if power, or money, satisfied him most, he replied "Neither; rather my work in the Sunday School". Finally, remember this man's mills fed us when Britain was blockaded during two world wars.

Boring sermons, and the burgeoning cinema led Arthur Rank to make short scriptural films for his Sunday School. Although amateurish, the teaching value was obvious. The idea of the Christian message on celluloid stimulated his father, who came up with a million pounds for starters! Miss Edith Carpenter tells me Mr. Rank insisted on productions comparable with secular films, and engaged well-known producers, actresses, and actors. His company 'Religious Films' was formed in 1933. Many well known stars today recall the caring atmosphere of the hostel he built for them. Some would join Mr. and Mrs. Rank in Sunday School where intruding pressmen got short shrift from the Superintendent.

Ministry of Information Films were made during the war. This architect of the British Film Industry conflicted with the distributors. "Not to worry" said hard-headed Joe, "We will distribute our own". The rest is history. Pinewood, Denham, Gaumont British, the Odeon chain with its top cinema in Leicester Square, scene of so many magnificent royal film premieres, home of the finest ever Compton Organ. King Arthur, as the film magnates called him, the man who realised one picture was worth a thousand words, kept up his work in Sunday School. The Ranks must have done more for Methodist Youth than any other family.

Bill Gowland also went into industry, albeit from another angle. In 1935 he raced around the Isle of Man, not in the T.T., but as a Methodist Minister, caring for seven churches. Fired with the spirit of John Wesley years later, he was picked with other top men for a Christian Commando team. They spoke at seasides, bomb sites, factory canteens etc. These operations were backed up with one of the five coach built mobile daylight cinemas purchased through the Rank Trust. Rank evangelism was now on wheels, and toured the U.K. and Channel Islands. Bill Gowland recalls the electrically raised hood, screen, and platform, from which he would not preach, but relate to the crowds, as only Bill could.

Not since John Wesley intervened in the Truro bread famine had Methodism done much more about works and workers. Instinctively, Bill felt called to break this virgin ground.

In 1954 he asked for a church with no future. He left his 1,500 congregation in Manchester, and came to Chapel Street, Luton, where 2,000 empty seats and £30,000 of dry rot awaited him. By taking a sledge hammer to the Victorian gas standards for scrap, Bill laid the first brick in his bridge between pew and pavement! - font and factory! Now Lord Rank had learned his milling round the corner at William Looker's Mill in Church Street, Luton, and Bill turned to him with a £26,000 plan to make a Community Centre from the derelict Sunday School building. Lord Rank came up with £20,000, and Bill with £25, yet a fourteen department hall and super youth facility emerged, where our Youth Club enjoyed many a "Saturday night in Luton". The full blown Industrial College was born in 1957 in a dirty room with twenty odd tables and chairs, and for ten years 6,000 people came on Industrial Chaplaincy Courses. A team of ladies fed them by day on one old gas stove, and Margaret and Roy Barrett found the local hospitality homes. The Gowland plan had proved its point. Exhausted, Bill turned again to Lord Rank with a £90,000 plan of the unique eight storey building that serves Methodism to this day.

"But we are closing colleges" protested Lord Rank. As for Bill, he had a £7,000 debt, but more faith than the Ranks had money, which was quite a lot. The outcome was `5,000 from the Chapel Fund, £40,000 from a Rank Trust Fund, £40,000 from Lord Rank, who had arranged the lot. Could this doyen of the silver screen have had a premonition of the 36,000 students destined to pass through the hands of Principal Reverend William Gowland during 35 years? For the uninformed, Bill Gowland is the 'Henry Giles' or 'Reginald Foort' of Methodism. The mighty oak or WurliTzer was not his vocation. Commending the Gospel is the gift thousands will remember him for.

The Ranks went out into a secular world and played the markets the Christian way. Exactly 100 years on from the birth of the - 'Good for Nowt Lad' - a 'Good for Nowt Church' - was transformed into a unique place of evangelism by two Sunday School Teachers' money.

What a combination - Capitalism and Christianity!

This Ford V8 was used extensively in rural areas across the UK in the 1950s. If the current Home Missions Dept's videos succeed in evangelizing like the films of the 1950s, Methodism's future is assured.

Believed Bedford-based, this mobile cinema used a 16mm carbon/arc rear projector and each unit had its own inbuilt generator. The driver/operator was employed by Home Missions.

The long wheelbase van on the right was pride of the fleet. A 35mm carbon/arc sound projector showed forward onto a mechanically raised hooded screen behind the cab. Likewise a platform lift rose for speakers.

Robert Gilmour LeTourneau was born in 1888 in Vermont, U.S.A. The fourth of eight children, Bob grew up in a strict Christian home, where he was restless, inquisitive, and ambitious. In between taking a correspondence course in algebra, geometry and engineering, he slogged away at wood cutting. This bought him a share in a small garage, where he excelled in oxy-acetylene welding.

In World War One, he served in a naval electric plant, gaining insight into generators for battleships.

Returning to his garage post war, his partner revealed the business had gone bankrupt. To pay off his debts Bob turned to tractor repairs. His first job was on a Holt tractor, where the timing had been fixed so often the locking device drifted in a moment. This had him retiming and spot welding, fixed for all time. Word and work spread from farm to farm. Bob, now a sturdy six footer, stood by "an intimidated" business man, and became a kind of minder to him. He courted his 17 year old daughter, Evelyn, and in the absence of permission, eloped 400 miles to Mexico to marry.

Bob bought a scrapped Holt tractor and scraper, repairing and working it a 10 hour day, to pay for it. This man broke the tradition of cast iron scrapers for all time, with his first lighter, stronger, all steel welded machine, built with Evelyn's help, in his driveway (between raising their children). Running out of cash and welding rods simultaneously, Bob remembered their curtain rods were bronze, and finished the job with them! Nicknamed the one tool, mechanic Bob welded an all steel workshop.

The couple's upbringing had much to do with them dedicating their lives to the Christian way of life and they pledged a portion of their regular income to God's work. This vibrant young couple's exuberance for life knew no bounds. Bob had no time for cant and humbug within the organised church and took his Bible literally. "Oh my God" coming from him was no casual exclamation but rather the opening request for help on some problem, perhaps a tractor on which he sought divine guidance. On offering himself as a missionary, he was told God needs business men like you to make money and fund them. He prayed "Prosper us, God, and the money is yours". His factories opened as other closed during the great Depression. In 1935 he and Evelyn set up a Christian Foundation into which 90% of their wealth went. In the office a card read "NOT HOW MUCH DO WE GIVE - HOW MUCH OF GOD'S MONEY DO WE KEEP?" Make of this what you like, but these committed Christians, and their family, really did make millions of pounds.

Bob's garage partnership had cost him the sale of 100 cord of hand cut wood. His first ever invention was a cable controlled butterfly valve, fitted beside a hole he cut in a car exhaust pipe ahead of the silencer, which when opened, gave a little extra power, and the roar of a train! This brought him popularity from 'Hot-rodders', and the opposite from residents. They landed the agency for 'Regal' cars, but couldn't afford the stand fee at a show. Bob got a free spot by building a 30ft high stairway, the width of the car, and without side safety rails, drove it back and forth three times a day.

When the lady wives of top officials visited a town's new LeTourneau factory site, Bob directed them to Evelyn, snaking beams off a truck with their old Chev. pick-up. Already she drove a truck and 24ft long trailer Bob had built her, just to collect children around town for Sunday School. Bob loved his youth work at the mission, and reluctantly left a major design problem, that had cost him days, to attend. He tells how in the midst of all the banter and noise, God revealed the design of his tractor scraper control unit, that was to lead all others for the next 25 years. By 1944, R.G.L. was building half of the world's earth moving equipment. In fact, they built over half of the U.S.A.'s muck shifting machines in World War Two. Bob had no time for Hitler, or anyone else that set themselves up as God!, and said so.

The U.S. Air Force approached Bob about a gigantic crane. In just two months he designed and delivered a 90 ton Cummins 335 H.P. crane that would pick up and carry a loaded 50 ton Liberator Bomber. One factory blacked out half the town, until Bob coupled eight big Cat. engines in synchronisation to a massive generator.

In 1946, now sponsoring Christian work across the world, Evelyn and Bob were flying over a 162 acre vacated Army Hospital at Long View, Texas, when divine inspiration led them to buy it. Here they established a Technical Institute to serve the many G.I.s returning from the war. Seven thousand passed through until 1961. Today it has become a Christian non-denominational college for 1,000 students in engineering, and various subjects. In 1947 Bob went to the U.S.A.'s version of 'Ruddington', and bought a war surplus Douglas A.26 Bomber he adapted as a 320 m.p.h. flying office. Now he could fly round the world and speak to business and churchmen alike, generally about eight times a weekend. At the World Trade Conference in 1951, Bob ruffled a few feathers with his "People want work, not handouts" talk.

Riding on 10 feet high tyres, one man operated, this 200 feet long earth scraper would scoop up 120 tons. Eight giant engines developed 5,000 h.p. This and other monsters were designed by Bob with God in mind. Photograph courtesy of Russell Jones.

In Liberia and Peru he leased half a million acres of jungle. Each project was pioneered
by a son or daughter. Bob's giant machines cleared the area, cropped it, and built villages.
A LeTourneau 10ft diameter tree-saw spinning at 170 m.p.h. with a pusher boom, and a 'tree
stinger' that rooted and exerted a quarter of a million pound heave 40 feet up, were with
other land juggernauts operated by men who were required to know their machines and their
Bibles. "You've not seen my machines" replied Bob, to the anxious native who said "You've
not seen the size of our trees". Today, thousands of people testify to the great lives of Evelyn
and Bob LeTourneau. I'm proud to have driven the first 'Tournapull' that came to Britain,
whilst in the Army, and I corresponded with R.G.L. in person in the 1950s. "No job is too
big. It's just our machines are too small", he would say. Of life's problems, he claimed, "none
are too large", it's just our thinking on them is too small"! Just imagine this man tackling
world starvation, unemployment, or even AIDS.

God gave him a brilliant intellect, inventive talent, and the ability to make money, with
the grace to use it justly. Yet his greatest attribute was humility. He never ended a talk
without saying "I'm only a mechanic that God has blest".

This man made millions to the Glory of God.

EDWIN

I heard some fascinating experiences from Edwin Foden's granddaughter, 90-year-old
Mrs. Doris Firth, the oldest surviving member of the Foden family, whom I traced in 1987.
Doris, incidentally, has a Bible, presented to her mother and father, Mr. and Mrs. S. P.
Twemlow, when they were married by the officers of Sandbach Wesleyan Sunday School.

Edwin Foden was born into a Methodist family in 1841, in the hamlet of Smallwood near
Sandbach. Not only the Gospel, but industriousness and diligence were preached in this
little chapel, and this is known to have characterised Edwin's life and accounted for his
capacity for hard work. Later at Mount Pleasant Methodist Church at Elworth, where he
would sit beside the clock, he was one of the first members, and his eldest son William was
the first to be married there. Edwin gave the building fund £1,000! Consider that sum then
against today's values, then consider what his capital must have been, and you have some
concept of this man's dedication to make money for Methodism.

Edwin led a committee to find and finance an organ for his Church. Prior to this,
congregational singing was led by a Cello, Clarinet, 2 Cornets, and a Serpent (now an
obsolete bass instrument). After work, music was Edwin's great love. At a Church meeting
it was decided to form a band. Later this became The Elworth Brass Band with 22 players.
On the occasion of Edward VII's Coronation they led a torch-light procession and showed
an improved repertoire. By June 1902 many of the players were Foden workers. Edwin
offered to take over the band, which became 'The Foden Silver Band'. Every concert would
close with 'Abide with Me', Edwin's favourite hymn. The Mortimers were Methodists, and
kept Elworth Post Office, and the hymn was changed when they took over the band
leadership. The rest is history.

When aged 7 years, Doris remembers a Sunday School treat to Congleton, when
grandad Foden first laid on steam waggons and trailers to transport them. Can you imagine
them all setting out in Sunday best white and returning smutty grey, and no 'New Bold' to
resort to!

After his clanking steam engines, what would Edwin have thought of this, the latest from the house of Foden? Not used for Sunday School treats, I presume. Photograph courtesy of John Cooper.

After this, the steamers and trailers became the regular transport for their treats and on them, beneath the Royal Coat of Arms read 'Steam Waggon Makers to H.M. The King'.

I understand King George sent a brace of pheasants to Foden's demonstrator at Sandbach.

Edwin Foden was a remarkable man of Motors, Music, and Methodism.

ROOTS OF METHODIST YOUTH

I chatted with a young preacher, Derrick Packman, of Lloyds Insurance of London, who told me the following facts.

A Methodist, Guy Chester, three times Deputy Chairman of Lloyds, had his own syndicate. This man renovated and placed a property in desirable Muswell Hill, London, at the disposal of Methodism. In 1947 he added other adjoining houses with big gardens, and tennis courts. In 1960 he presented property to the local Manse. Guy's main dream was a residential hostel for the thousands of our young women and men who come to work in London. He gave the land, and donated the first £50,000 towards the £230,000 for the Methodist Youth House in Muswell Hill, a substantial centre that opened in 1960, originally catering for 88 young people. The property is also the Headquarters of the Methodist Association of Youth Clubs, an organisation that is still the envy of other denominations.

This great club movement is traced to the Rev. Jimmy Butterworth, whose brain-child was "Clubland", a building for deprived South London youth. This was near the former home of comedian Bob Hope, who was so impressed he donated a large sum of money for an imposing new building.

Paul Lang, Lord Rank's nephew reminds me that the dedication of the Rank fortunes to the use of God's work was exceptional.

Of course the Ranks, LeTourneaus and Chesters of this world are all too rare. Even so, thousands, indeed millions, give money and time sacrificially to numerous causes. Our founder, John Wesley, who logged 250,000 miles on horseback (not the same one - he got through over twenty) preaching the gospel across England said this: "Earn all you can - save all you can - give all you can". Our sometimes misunderstood ex president of the Methodist Conference, the Rev Richard Jones, says "Everything we have -money, property, talent and time - are God's gifts to us. Use what we must for ourselves, give as much as we possibly can to others". Now there's food for thought. This thinking is the life line to the needy and our great charities.

In 1928, a man named Newall lodged at 'Bramingham House', Eaton Bray. He drove a mobile daylight cinema, belonging to the 'Methodist Times' paper. A display on the Market Place at Eaton Bray was to be my first link with 'Motors' and 'Methodism'. Sunday School Superintendent Amos Cobb was pretty tough: an ex-Indian Army man, with a voice like thunder, used for public announcements long before 'Focus', our village magazine. This remarkable man collected, then sold, eggs and fruit 20 miles away in Watford. Loll Piggott recalled those twice weekly journeys with Amos and his horsedrawn four wheeled van and lurcher dog that trotted alongside. Claiming he feared no man, only God, Amos would set off on icy roads, perhaps walking and leading his horse the whole 40 miles in winter. On one occasion, the horse fell down, breaking one of the van's main shafts. As a temporary measure Loll purloined a clothes prop from a neighbouring garden, using it as a splint to repair the shaft. Amos returned it the following week to thank the benefactor, who was unaware of the help given.

Amos Cobb in Northall Road, Eaton Bray, as it used to be.

Connie Newman, Eaton Bray's first lady driver. Her father Charlie, staunch Methodist baker, gave loaves of bread to hungry families in the 1920s.

Arthur Holmes, still milking aged eighty four, delivered milk on his Rudge motorcycle and sidecar from a 12 gallon and 3 gallon churn. This man loaned me tractors for a pittance in the 1950s.

This stern disciplinarian commanded great respect from his Bible Class Lads. When he saw four of us awkwardly trying to 'chat up' two girls, his ensuing 'Birds and Bees' warning told of tarty women ready to drag a man to hell: "When courting, find out if she can cook. Avoid girls with nice hands. Go for ones stained from blacking the grate", this rare old patriarch advised. Eaton Bray's Salvation Army, founded in a barn, had a magnificent band. In 1936 a certain Captain White had the unique idea of combining P.T. with Youth work. My mother enrolled her youngest 'flabby' son. I featured in a display "Tumbling for Health and Strength". This led to much laughter and applause for all the wrong reasons. I invariably fouled the vaulting horse in the Army, the penalty for which required me to blanco the P.T. Corporal's Kit. I have hated athletics to this day.

Sunday School treats were great occasions. Others recall, but I can't, Blake's lorries

The boy at the door of this Pope charabanc in 1922 is Cyril Baines (now committed to serving the Senior Citizens). The outing was from North Street Methodist, now Trinity Church.

An Edlesborough choir outing to Windsor in a Blake charabanc.

loaded with Chapel forms on which the children sat. But Jim Bates' and others' waggonettes decorated with bracken from Ashridge, I do. Mr. Pope of Hockliffe once had two charabancs lined up outside the Chapel in torrential rain, destined for Bedford. Inside the chapel about sixty parents and children were praying for a safe journey and fine weather. Divine intervention unfortunately not being forthcoming, Mr. Pope offered to postpone the trip and return on a less inclement day without extra charge, which was done.

Tommy Blake was popular, as he would drive and sing. We once got up to "300 Men and their Dog - went to Mow a Meadow", returning from Kettering.

Best remembered coaches were George E. Costin's of Dunstable. George was well known for his horse hire. His fast white horses were on call to pull the Town's Fire Engine. During a 'flu' epidemic, two of these were blacked over for funeral work!

Three of George Costin's Brakes set off for a Weslyan outing. This man pioneered passenger transport hereabouts.

Four of Costins coaches parked up at Southend in 1938. This only photograph of the luxury AEC 'Regal' is not flattering to her but depicts members of the Methodist Sunday School alive today, 1990.

Various motor vehicles led to two new Albion Coaches being commandeered by the Army in 1939. Then the latest in luxury was an AEC Regal Coach. Under Arthur Costin, and his three sons, the Company expanded to fifteen coaches. When the firm was taken over in 1970, the fleet boasted three twin steer Bedford VAL 55 seaters: a most prestigious company in its day.

My abhorrence of alcohol germinated in 1932 when seven of my cousins were bereft of their father in a drink-related accident. The constant parental reminder of the perils of drink left me with a psychological barrier, that led to violent sickness after even sherry flavoured trifle at a Wedding! Doubtless the odd wine gum would lead to a positive breath test!

Therefore I sold organs uneasily to Inns. However, a 'pub' organist, Eric Brewer, demonstrated with positive success for us, and reminded landlords they made more on my soft drinks than beer. Eric's signature tune was "Moonlight and Roses", words now on his tombstone in Stewkley Churchyard. On a Saturday night a packed 'pub' of merry singers would stop sharp as he swung from "Nellie Dean" to "Abide with me" in foxtrot tempo, in a poignant kind of respect, and I once witnessed a drunk, who had been slurring every tune, sober up and sing three verses of this hymn with perfect diction. Some word had touched a memory, I presume. The popularity of "The Old Rugged Cross" also amazed me.

I write this in the old 'Bedford Arms' yard, now Roebuck Garage, as Nick James M.O.T.s my van. This was the site of old cottages that housed rough and tough deprived families. Midst the brawls and fights, a wire was stretched across the opening, intended to decapitate bicycle mounted 'bobbies' called to the fray. As each cottage became vacant, Mr. Wallace would buy it and demolish it. Appalled by the lack of wedlock, the Rev. Sutton (Vicar of Eaton Bray from 1890-1916) offered a free marriage service to the residents en masse.

Competing with 14 pubs, this man, with Mr. Wallace, had the Coffee Tavern built, with its fine billiard room above. Completed in 1901 at a cost of £1,000, Mr. Wallace anxiously queried the lack of stairs. Builder Jeffrey Sharrett, who disliked architects, simply explained, "Your man never drew stairs, so I didn't build any". Hence the exterior stairway to this day.

UNCLE JOE

My uncle, Joe Parkins of Dunstable, was one of the most enterprising pioneers of local motor haulage.

Backed by Builder's Merchant, Percy Lockhart, he bought a new Ford 'T' one tonner, lefthand drive U.S.A. produced chassis in 1920.

Carpenters Vic Field and Bill Webb (my old playmate's father), then of the Five Bells, Eaton Bray, built the body and cab; £240 the lot.

In between shovelling on and off loads of sand, my grandfather found him regular loads of eggs for London, at 15 m.p.h. flat out. My aunt Sis brought an inborn acumen for business to their marriage, and they met a new demand for Furniture Removals. First on was always the inverted large kitchen table onto the cab top. Chairs etc stacked between the legs gave a 'Luton Van' type appearance when the load was sheeted. Ten years later another Ford followed, then uncle designed his own body for a new Commer chassis. By now he was a nationwide removal man, and specialist in the transportation of antiques for the well known Rixson Brothers.

A great believer in a well loaded tailboard, during the war he was directed to transport laundry for Charing Cross Hospital, at that time transferred to Ashridge House.

Joe Parkins USA-built 1920 T Ford. Livestock, sand, furniture… he carried it all.

The Commer 'Centaur'. Its semi Luton body was designed by the owner. In the week he carried priceless antiques, on Sundays a penetrating message from the pulpit.

Uncle Joe did much to foster my boyish interest in lorries and took me many a mile before his retirement in 1962. In 1984 he was invited to a Buckingham Palace Garden Party, in recognition of his services to Methodism. Being an ardent Youth Worker and a local preacher for 64 years blended with his success in business.

Years ago, three teenaged girls responded to this man's forceful preaching. One of these was to have a daughter, Margaret, and another a son, John. These two 14-15-year olds, together with another girl named Enid, became the founder members and the rockbed of our pioneering project, the Youth Club. Methodism was born 'in song', and music features high with its Youth. One stranded vehicle I winched out with my Latil, at a wet Eaton Bray Traction Engine Rally, was Garth Holman's artic low loader and Fowler engine, grossing at 22 tons. It transpired his children, Heather aged 12, and Jack aged 8, were ardent organists. Both blossomed in the Bletchley Yamaha Music School, one of the national network of organ teaching centres set up by Kemble Yamaha, through Len Rawle, director of music teaching. No other manufacturer has done more for teaching all ages, hence their continued lead in U.K. sales. At the Bedford South Sunday School Eistedfodd, Heather and Jack have each won the cup for most points in their age group. The test was on a 'heavy going' Pipe Organ. Perched on the seat edge, Jack could just touch the pedals. His set piece was 'Going Home', the Hovis advert's tune.

Our early Sunday School music involved a great deal of singing, especially for the Anniversary, when "Grandpa King" of Totternhoe, a nearby village, would come over to conduct.

Nowadays we have the skills of three brilliant young lady wind instrumentalists and recorder players, who are such a credit to teacher, Jean Carter, to enliven our special services.

I tire of those who question the role of Women Ministers of Religion. The Rev. Nichola Jones came to us like the breath of a force nine gale! Good at visiting, as well as good in the pulpit, superb with youth, this "dashing daughter of Wesley" spoke to 10,000 young people who packed the Royal Albert Hall in 1987.

One criteria, overlooked by top clergy in this controversial issue, is the female reaction to 'a mouse in the pulpit'. I happen to know that Nichola endured even this situation, with courage!!

On demobilisation in 1946, I was concerned about the lack of week night activities for the youth of our Church.

Together with my cousin, Sheila Hebbes, and the sisters Mary and Kathleen Croxford, we formed the first Youth Club in the entire district, which I was privileged to lead for 14 years.

The highlights were Hostel Weekends, in a converted redundant Chapel, at aptly named Cupid Green, near Hemel Hempstead in Hertfordshire, and annual visits to the Albert Hall, London, for the Methodist Association of Youth Clubs' weekends, acknowledged as one of the biggest (20,000 strong) religious gatherings of youth in Europe. Astonished Church Elders first opposed my idea of Sunday films, but we packed them in, young and old alike. The large sums of charity money raised by enthusiastic Club members was phenomenal.

Forty years on, in 1986, Peter Mayne put on a slide show of Club nostalgia for me. Word got to ex Club members, who came in droves from a hundred miles or more. After fond farewells, a deputation called, as I prepared for bed. "Could we have a reunion"? they enquired. Ten local ex Club members, and one amazing fellow from Kent, who traversed the M25 many times, formed a committee, and in April 1988 we relived the 1950s and 60s in one almighty knees-up.

I was literally speechless when an inscribed watch was presented to me. Believe me, there is no better investment of one's spare time than in young people. The dividends are high indeed.

Our Youth Club Reunion, 1988. Left to right: Linda Potton, Iris Hignell, Rev Nichola Jones and Angela Rose. To meet men last seen in short trousers and women now grandmothers was emotionally demanding. Few are as privileged to see the fruits of their efforts as this.

NEWS FLASH

Eaton Bray Methodist Church – built 1795 – threatened in 1990. We've got dry rot! £35,000 wanted and sponsoring for Nichola Jones who has agreed to drive Tony Potton's 25 ton, 285 hp, 10 feet wide "Mighty Antar" gigantic recovery truck. *CAN SHE DO IT???*
Put your money on her and assist CORDA as well.

Postscript:
HEARTFELT THANKS

In 1984, without the slightest warning, whilst felling a tree, I keeled over. My hands were powerless to stop the chainsaw running beside me. Nature had chosen this moment to announce I had incurable heart disease. As an E.C.G. machine churned out its grim verdict, my ticker was surging like a Perkins P.6 diesel. The thought 'so this is death' came upon me and I thought of things I'd have done differently in my life if I had my time over again.

Ten days in Brompton Heart Hospital, London, that great Cathedral of Cardiology, was an education. In Queen Victoria's time tuberculosis was the rampant killer. When a solicitor found no London hospital would admit his stricken staff, he gathered friends, raised money, and Brompton, initially as a Chest Hospital, was born. I've seen tired nurses and doctors form a team and rush to respond to a cardiac arrest call. Having secured their goal there was no hugging, autograph hunters, or a million pound transfer offer from another hospital. Just the pittance we pay these people since they only save life and are not of entertainment value. Scattered round the walls of the hospital church are plaques to the memory of a host of young nurse T.B. victims, inscribed 'Died at their Post'. In gratefulness I pledged the days I was to be spared to fund raising for the heart charity, CORDA, that was funding the unique Magnetic Resonance Scanner, that photographs the heart between beats. My first £400 came from sales of an audio tape of characters and timber vehicles. I got sponsors for everything, cassettes, even packaging - the lot. For many days Organ Recordist Bill Ravenall edited and copied every tape. Not being able to afford background music copyright fees, I turned to Len Rawle for automated music. What he came up with was a thrilling March dedicated to CORDA which he composed and recorded on a huge Yamaha Organ. I have pledged my net profits of my last book to CORDA, but by far the major amount of the £4,000 plus I have raised comes from the tremendous efforts of Mary and Peter Mayne, who have put on various nostalgic events relating to Eaton Bray, and donations in memory of friends and loved ones. Veteran of the CORDA Management, Professor Donald Longmore, F.R.C.S., divulged his dream to me four years ago. It was detection, through mass public screening, from mobile diagnostic units. He envisaged a 'Rapide' type of six wheeled coach-like vehicle, with a $6^1/2$ ton magnet amidships, centrally linked to computers.

Tuberculosis was overcome by mass screening with the old Leyland Beaver X Ray units. CORDA is now set to lead the way of mass eradication of heart disease. At last these vehicles are nearing reality. I yearn to see the first, offering life for millions previously unaware they face death. To all who have supported CORDA through my encouragement, THANK YOU. Please keep it up, we are on the way.

Remember CORDA work covers the whole spectrum of life, from children with congenital heart disease upwards.

There are only two full time staff at CORDA: Executive Director Anthony Burns and assistant Sheila James, who have infectious enthusiasm and drive that has inspired me and this charity's success to date.

Most charities come to us with problems. CORDA is different: it comes with an answer. We only need the money.

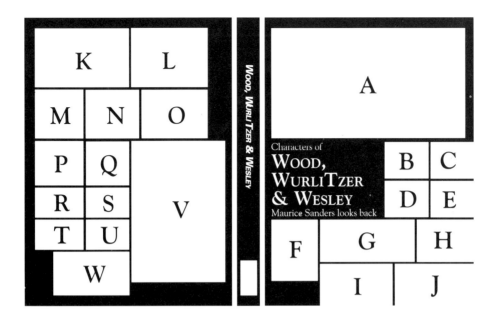

Key to Cover photographs

Front Cover:

A The Marvelous Mann
B Foort chose Commer
C Bert Imber battles on!
D Croasdales in Cumbria, 1930s
E Ben Minto's TD6
F Engine man Brown of High Wycombe
G Later shortened into a tractor
H Methodist Outreach, 1950s
I Potter's War Office secret
J Laura, Reuben, Rosa and Shirley

Back Cover:

K Somewhere in Durham
L Loading a pole-buster!
M A favourite Volvo flatbed
N Luton's first Fodens
O 'Holt' – the forerunner of Caterpillar
P Rafting in Loch Monar
Q Ex Cooper, Ex Garham, today Exceptional
R Bullocks in the Black Forest
S My £3 Austin 7
T A Midland Matador
U Fodens for ever
V A Baillie Matador conversion
W 'This is the answer' – local artist Ian King

Acknowledgement

Some of the facts on pages 175-177 come from *Mover of Men and Mountains*, R.G.Le Tourneau's autobiography. Available in the UK from Sunday School Union House, 130 City Road, London EC1V 2NJ. I also acknowledge the help of Richard Fowler of the Le Tourneau College, Texas.